Saving America Now

The Buffet Syndrome
Expanded Edition

Ron Slover

Path Publishing

Amarillo, Texas

Path Publishing
4302 SW 51st #121
Amarillo, Texas 79109-6159
USA
Path@PathPublishing.com
PathPublishing.com

Cover by Path Publishing and CreateSpace
Eagle art by Adexim.com

To contact the author or order copies, see About the Author and the Publisher at the end of the book.

ISBN-13: 978-1502893178
ISBN-10: 1502893177

Printed in the United States of America

Dedications

This book is dedicated to the people — including entire families — who have given up on America. Those are the people who are tired of witnessing and listening to constant bickering, empty promises, lines of baloney, creative back-stabbing, and the never ending attempts to divide our people. It is those many millions of good Americans who have seen the failure of programs, which were developed supposedly to help society, that have left them in despair and in conflict with themselves, their families, communities, and nation — all the while not understanding what has actually happened.

Then to those people who realize that no matter what they do, how many taxes they pay, how much red tape and bureaucracy they contend with or how well they plan for the future, the cards are stacked against them — and in the end, things only get worse.

And the people who realize that the system that created a great America has been greatly diminished. People want to see a national environment in which there is mutual respect and encouragement for all citizens, while all exercise responsibility and take chances to succeed.

Finally, this book is dedicated to all the citizens of America: the perceived rich and poor, and the middle class, and all racial and ethnic minorities. The one thing many citizens have in common is a total disgust for the behavior and game-playing by many of our so-called national leaders, in both the U.S. House and Senate.

Note to Readers

The words in this font, Garamond, are from the original 2007 *The Buffet Syndrome*.

Words in this font, Calibri, are the words added in 2014 to create *Saving America Now.*

Contents

Our younger generations, ages 5 through 50, always need to be aware of the opportunities in America. They must appreciate the fact that working hard, getting an education, accepting responsibility, being creative and seeking job opportunities create pride and self-respect for themselves and their families. That attitude is what results in the success of America and its people.

Ron Slover

Foreword

When compared with the total period of time in which America has existed as a nation, seven years is a very small fraction of our history, yet much has occurred since the publication of *The Buffet Syndrome*. *Saving America Now* updates important events, politics, economic trends, and the very real danger facing Americans.

It's hard for me to believe what seven short years have done to this nation. When the Declaration of Independence was signed in 1776, America began to be transformed into what became the envy of the world, surpassing nations that had existed for hundreds and even thousands of years. Unfortunately, so much has changed.

Let's go now to the start of the foreword in *The Buffet Syndrome.*

America is considered the most powerful nation in the world. The quality of life in America, as a general rule, is envied by most other nations. To people in many other countries we certainly would appear to be the luckiest, wealthiest, and even the most blessed people on Earth.

There is no shortage of "experts" or "authorities" — some good and some bad — on hundreds of subjects many Americans deal with. It seems that most books about these matters include more than the subject or problem being presented. The author's expertise in how to work out a problem is always a significant part of the book, even to the point where the subject being discussed becomes extremely complex.

The same problem or subject might have already been unsuccessfully dealt with by hundreds, or even thousands of other experts or authorities. How is it then that any writer, all by himself, can have all the answers to a complex issue? The answer is simple. He has an opinion, perhaps based on knowledge, evidence, scientific reasoning, or what-have-you, but in the final analysis, it is still his opinion. He might be totally correct in his solution to a problem or an issue, but is that solution actually workable or realistic?

It is my opinion that just understanding *why* a problem exists, especially if it is a serious matter, becomes most important. There is no simple answer to something that is vitally important to us Americans, especially when most of the factors contributing to the complexity of an issue are beyond the direct control of any one of us.

Yes, America is a great nation, but it has huge economic, social, and political problems. Monumental problems that cannot be dealt with, corrected, or eliminated unless we understand *why* we are in the mess we are in.

All I want to do is discuss some ideas about issues that are causing America to be less than its potential. With information, we will be better equipped to make plans on how to prepare ourselves and our families for our probable future.

If I repeat myself in places, it is because what I am repeating is very important. It's like my doctor, who may say the word "inflammation" several times in describing my physical condition as he encourages me to improve my diet by eating fewer fatty foods and get more exercise. In this book, I am trying to get government waste and bureaucracy out of our national system to restore financial health through personal responsibility!

Unlike some other authors, I just happen to believe that most people in this country, when faced with the realities of life, take the responsibility to do what is best for themselves, their families, and even their country. We only have one opportunity on this Earth to live our lives happily and enjoy a nation that still offers opportunity to those who pursue it. We should never underestimate ourselves as a people, even though many of our so-called leaders give us little credit for having the ability to accomplish anything significant on our own.

Wouldn't it be nice to read a book about extremely important issues, yet written in everyday language with clear ideas? For a change, how about a common sense discussion we can all relate to that evaporates all the smokescreens, allowing us to finally make a rational analysis?

Here is another novel idea: Why not allow the reader to form an opinion for himself or herself?

It seems that most articles, statements, or writings of any sort in which the writer or spokesperson is trying to make a point, presents only his opinion. For a dynamic change, why not present some facts and opinions, in terms anyone can understand, and honestly ask the reader to form their own opinion? So I try to set aside many technical terms, deal with the political realities that exist in America today, and analyze the huge issues that we must deal with, now and in future years.

I think it is healthy for people to think for themselves. Thus, what you will be reading in these pages are facts based on history, reality, national trends, motivations, predictable politics, and responses to various situations which have been presented to the American people and our leaders. While I have also included my own opinions, I encourage independent thought.

Although America is a nation with huge structural, political, and economic challenges, my great hope is that national leaders of both political parties finally become honest with the people.

But this isn't just a book about governing the nation. More importantly, it is about how we respond to the society we live in and our government. It is about a national system that is hopelessly dysfunctional in dealing with a significant percentage of its population, people who are helping to ensure its ultimate failure.

Because of the subjects I discuss, it is safe to say I will make more enemies than friends. Liberals, conservatives, Republicans, Democrats, politicians, bureaucrats, the young, the old, the rich, the poor, elected leaders even at the local level, and many professional people with very impressive degrees are likely to be upset. They may be upset because I am commenting on extremely important and personal issues that threaten the credibility of many people and will hopefully influence the economic and social future of America.

It won't take long for the reader to fully understand the title of this book and see how the term "Buffet Syndrome" applies to hundreds of situations involving the United States and its people.

While America during the past several decades, and probably for over a century, has been considered the most powerful nation in the world, that is no longer true.

How does a nation gain "most powerful" status? Many people relate it to being militarily the strongest nation. Others think of it as being the most economically sound. And most likely people in many nations continue to view America as being a land of economic opportunity, with freedom, new technologies, and power still invested in the people. And yes, while remaining the strongest military force on the earth.

Yet, in all honesty, if we relate most powerful status to being economically strong enough to develop and maintain the most sophisticated military force in the world, that is no longer true. In my opinion, almost within the blink of an eye, in historical terms, the world has changed its opinion of America.

This may come as a real shock to most Americans today, but in my opinion the world doesn't respect or fear America's military power. It all boils down to this: It doesn't matter how large, how sophisticated, how damaging, how precise, how widespread an area it covers, or how expensive our military is if we don't have the national commitment to use it when necessary.

Please recall how wars were fought in the past, such as World War I and World War II. We didn't have the sophisticated weapons we have today. There were battles where large artillery pieces were aimed at a general area rather than precise targets. Our troops in foxholes fired at enemy troops in foxholes and perhaps bunkers. We had ships that fired into foxholes or bunkers.

It's important that we remember one wartime term: "carpet bombing." Without the sophisticated weaponry that is now in the possession of several nations today, there was absolutely no choice but to spread destruction over a wide area in order to achieve a military victory. Whether it was light, medium, or heavy bombers, or aircraft firing 50-caliber bullets and dropping bombs on targets, nations had to win using these far from sophisticated weapons on targets that they hoped were enemies.

So what are we doing today? This nation is obsessed with not inflicting what's being referred to as "collateral damage," what some would call unnecessary damage. How is it that we can be in military conflict with a nation, and its leaders, but must limit our attacks to a single sophisticated weapon landing on a specific site? I will never forget the number of times I watched the national news during the Iraq conflict and saw a pile of rubble with a teddy bear placed on it in a prominent position. Other nations look at our massive military capability yet know full well that we don't have the will to use it.

In the ninth paragraph of the 2007 foreword I stated, "I just happen to believe that most people in this country, when faced with the realities of life, take the responsibility to do what is best for themselves, their families, and even their country." The question is, has that changed during the past seven years? That statement is still basically true, but what has changed is that we have never been a more divided country than we are today. What we find in the year 2014 is that an even larger percentage of the nation's population does not take responsibility to do what is best for themselves, their families or their country.

While we have become more aware of the unfunded liabilities we face, the fact that the number of people on food stamps has doubled, that there is no Social Security Trust Fund, that the national debt has doubled, that in four of the past seven years we have had deficits of more than one trillion dollars, and there's now even more people that just don't care.

Our national leaders are talking about "economic justice," "social justice," and various kinds of "rights." Many organizations have been formed to carry these messages to the people — all growing at a pace so fast that it's almost unimaginable, during a period of time in which we are witnessing a dramatic increase in rules, regulations, policies, budgets, and regulatory agencies.

Still another topic of discussion that has now started taking place is what one could call state subjugation to the federal government. We are nation composed of 50 states, and for the most part, Americans consider themselves to be not only Americans but residents of a state. I like to think of myself as being a Texan, and I'm proud of being a Texan, proud of my state.

But what bothers me is that we have begun hearing discussions, statements, declarations or what-have-you from some of our so-called leaders which boil down to this: Any issue that involves both federal and state authority has now suddenly come under federal authority.

There is no way that I will ever accept the theory that federal authority always supersedes any and all state authority. For the life of me, I simply can't understand how we as a nation, composed of people who consider themselves residents of their states, can ever passively accept such a theory.

Thus I have outlined some of the many problems we face in this country. What I intend to do in this book is to further define and enlarge upon the issues and give solutions where I can.

Chapter 1

America, a Divided Nation

It is impossible to establish a real picture of what America is today without seriously analyzing what makes the nation function, or in many cases, what makes it fail to function.

In order for any person in this country to make a rational, sincere, and very objective judgment of our federal government and its relationship to the people, some serious thought must be dedicated to the process.

Compared to many other nations of the world, some with a history of thousands of years, the U.S. is the new kid on the block. Having amazed those other countries with our accomplishments in such a short period of time, we must face the reality that much of their admiration of us has faded.

We would all like to believe that we have the strongest economy in the world, the finest military, and are the greatest example of democracy in the world. We portray Americans as a people enjoying freedom and participating in our capitalist system.

I would like to think that all this is true. It certainly was true for many decades. We still have the strongest military force in the world. In reality, our military force and economic security are taking a backseat to other programs in the U.S. Those other programs are being showered upon us at the expense of our national security and the economic security of the nation.

The economy of the U.S. is perceived as being very

strong. However, what's perceived and what's true are different. Because of politics in the U.S. (of which both political parties are guilty), the long-term economic outlook for the U.S. is grim at best. The chances of it surviving a downturn — that we can't even begin to imagine, due to its severity — are *almost nil*.

America's free enterprise system for many decades has created economic opportunity for millions of people. Capitalism has almost become a dirty word in our world today, and unfortunately, many of our political leaders are helping to undermine the American free enterprise system. Much of the media helps those politicians condemn our capitalist system. It's strange that the same media will praise a rising Dow Jones average while simultaneously condemning companies and individuals for making money. They claim that the money is being taken from the poor or that the wealth isn't being shared more equally.

People come to America sometimes through necessity, and other times by choice. Whether it's a refugee family fleeing an oppressive government or someone simply thinking America is a better place to be, there are generally two factors they find attractive: opportunity and freedom.

The word "freedom" is a touchstone to most Americans. The state of being free, for the most part, is taken for granted because we are Americans. We have always been free, ever since we declared our freedom centuries ago. We not only declared our freedom as a nation, but we fought hard for that freedom. Yet I predict that at some point in time, based upon history, economics, politics, greed, expansion of power, survival, and even a little pure hate, our status of being free as we know it today will come to an end.

Our economic problems, as well as other major problems that we in the U.S. simply refuse to deal with, are caused by the most pressing problem in our nation today: political dishonesty. When I say political dishonesty, it is important that the reader understands exactly what I mean.

Let's assume that all politicians are, in fact, 100 percent

honest, both legally and morally. But the problem is that we have a federal system in which there are issues not being dealt with that are vitally important to the people, like the economy and the future of this nation. Politicians just simply refuse to present, *to disclose,* true facts to the American people.

For example, why in the world would a federal politician use a term like "Trust Fund" when discussing the huge problem of Social Security? Why are we even talking about the possibility of a balanced budget? Politicians should understand that the American people, because of the proud history of this country, can deal with almost anything if their leaders are honest with them.

This is the situation we have today, and nothing is more important than the fact that we as a people are not being given the true picture of what is really happening in America or of the financial obligations of the U.S. We need to have full disclosure if we are going to deal with the massive problems that will soon overtake us.

How can I say that America is a divided nation? Well, in reality we are. We are a divided nation governed by politicians and operated by a bureaucracy. A bureaucracy can be further defined as an administration characterized by excessive waste, red tape, routine, and programs of questionable value. There are many reasons why we are divided and, unfortunately, nearly all have to do with the politics involved.

We obviously are divided by race. Politicians always want us to be cognizant that there are multiple races, and that we have a racial problem. We are divided by economics, especially by the economics within the "classes" of people: the poor, the wealthy, the super rich, and the great middle class. We are also divided by age, from teens to senior citizens.

We are seriously divided by the basic concepts of the political parties, whether Democrats or Republicans, or the liberals versus the conservatives. The fringe elements of each party should be properly called "fringe" rather than being associated with a particular philosophy or party. They are out in fields all by themselves, groups that generally have several key opinions, all set in stone with no thought-out rationale as to why the opinions exist. What we have is a situation in which we continue on a daily basis to divide people for political purposes in order to aid politicians in their desire to perpetuate themselves in office. Since we are a seriously divided nation, if we don't deal with our problems we are going to become even more divided. By not dealing with major problems, life in America can only get worse.

Since most people would agree with me that America is divided, one question to ask is, "What means are used to divide our people?" There are several ways this is done.

While most Americans are unaware of this, there has been a successful marketing plan underway for many years, promoted by thousands of people, organizations, political groups, vested interests, and even the media, all intent on dividing America every day. Whatever their reasons, and the reasons vary greatly, they do not want us to feel like we are a united people, under God or any other ideal.

Remember this though: The stakes are very high and the people involved are dedicated to succeeding in their goals. By dividing us, and encouraging us to believe that we are involved in a life or death struggle against each other where each of us has to win at all costs, the nation is in a constant state of turmoil, has changed from what made it a great nation, and is quite possibly beyond repair.

Let's look at several of the most important tactics or conditions that have divided America and see how people have responded in large numbers. Keep in mind that some of these have been underway for many years, an almost daily barrage of ideas, allegations, philosophies, and intentional game playing that has brainwashed the public into accepting them as not only correct but irrefutable.

The number one reason we have become divided, which we should keep in mind when discussing the others, is political posturing. As national politicians engage in this perpetual political posturing, there is never a message being delivered to the people about what makes America a great country.

To counter this destructive trend, we have also elected leaders who have pride in the role they play, have real principles, care about America, are committed to working in the best interests of the nation, and still believe in America's free enterprise system and the people who make the system work.

Yet many national political campaigns are totally phony. One has only to casually observe campaigns and listen to what is discussed. Most of the banter is a constant stream of allegations against some group or some proposal, along with promises to change that situation to some other group's economic advantage.

For example, in almost every race, a candidate — either the candidate holding the office at the time or a contender for the office — always attempts to discredit the other party to gain support for their philosophy. The opponent's position is not in the best interest of any group he is trying to get votes from. Declaring that an opponent is dead wrong is in itself an intentional plan to divide people. Once people have fully accepted the fact that being politically aware means that Americans must be divided into special interest groups, further division of our people is much easier.

America is divided by economics. The average American can look around his community, his state, and his country and see wide variations in wealth. Expensive houses and far less expensive houses, good parts of town and bad parts, new cars and old cars, people dressed in suits and people wearing little more than rags.

As people observe their status in life compared to others, it is a natural response for them to see themselves in an economic group, a racial group, a work group — with whatever groups they associate themselves. They find out that we don't all have the same assets. In America we have the extremely rich, the incredibly poor, and everything in between

— even great differences within families.

When we add the political ingredient to the subject of economic division, things become distorted. The truth is that it is virtually impossible to put the American people into two categories: rich and poor. Though we hear those words from Washington every day, only a very tiny group can be defined as rich and a tiny group could be defined as poor. In other words, we could look at the absolute extremes on the wealth scale and have no question that a radical difference exists between the family with absolutely nothing and the family that possesses everything that could possibly be imagined.

My question is this: How do we classify the 98 percent in the middle? Should we call them rich or poor, or what? Perhaps a better question to ask is: What is the average American's economic level? And as we relate back to reason number one, politics, we hear national politicians make public statements every day referring to "the rich" or "the poor," very often implying that the poor are that way as a direct result of the rich being rich.

Since national politicians have had huge successes by claiming to be saviors of the poor from the hands of the rich, they have created another code phrase, "the middle class." This new group gives them fresh fodder every day. They now say they are concerned that the middle class is being hurt by the rich. Since it is hard to define what the average poor or average rich is, almost everybody winds up in the middle class.

The real effect of this political salvation is simply to give our federal government a green light to establish new or expanded programs and taxes. Sadly, millions of Americans actually believe that our government wants to tax the rich in order to protect the middle class. Some of our national leaders try to convince people that the "poor" and "middle class" can be assured of certain services they are entitled to, at the expense of the "rich," who could pay more taxes. In reality, it is impossible to define the middle class.

One thing is for sure, there will be more federal taxes

levied against more people in a much broader range of incomes — thus, more hypocrisy from many elected officials, bigger budgets, no spending discipline, and further divisions of people along economic lines.

The third most important reason why America is divided, unfortunately, is race. This *constant effort*, particularly by politicians, reminds us that we as a people are not the same. Every day on television when economic situations are discussed, someone points out that we are not economically the same and that we are not the same socially. It has become a common practice to conveniently inject the subject of race into economic comparisons, so we are being led to believe that economic differences are caused by racial differences.

A politician really likes telling this story, leading people to believe that the reason their economic position isn't the same as others is because of their race or unfair leverage by the rich. That means he has become the savior of the poor or middle class, whatever constitutes one or the other. And as savior, he is dividing Americans at every opportunity, simply to allow himself to gain or retain his position of power.

The fourth reason for such division existing in America is our national news media, which is very biased in its presentation. Some sources intentionally slant items to the left and some to the right; the majority, though, are left-leaning. Much more about the media is in a later chapter of this book. However, I need to say here that it is the media that delivers the messages of the politicians to America. So an elected official has a "forum" available to him, while the average citizen of this country does not. Most of us start forming opinions from, among other things, the media, which delivers the messages from the person who has the forum, the politician.

Thanks to the politicians and left-leaning media, we receive a constant barrage of stories *telling us* that we are different because, in some manner or other, some group is getting ripped off by some other group.

I find it interesting, and sometimes even amusing, that

there are so many "experts" in media broadcasting. The truth is that many of them are little more than stooges for the companies they work for, presenting the biased positions of their employers. I can't help but get amused when an "expert" doesn't know the difference between a million and a billion, or perhaps a billion and a trillion dollars. My question is this: How much of an expert is the television commentator or reporter or newspaper writer who doesn't know the difference in 100 million dollars and 100 billion dollars? How can he have the common sense to tell us what is important?

The media and the politicians feed each other. The media likes attacks. If someone, including a national political leader, wanted to say we are a great nation whose people work hard, want to achieve goals in their lives, are proud of themselves and their communities, and have the desire to accept responsibility for their lives, that won't fit any media agenda. The media doesn't consider that a story. They, like politicians, report attacks.

I want to relate a personal story that shows what can happen after America is bombarded over a period of years by politicians using economics and race as issues to gain power or retain power, with their message delivered by a biased media. This is a great example of using economics and race to distort reality.

I recall an incident during a political campaign I was involved in more than 20 years ago. The event was an open political forum that included both Democrats and Republicans.

Some candidates were present while other candidates had a spokesperson representing them. The question I was asked offered me the opportunity to publicly COMMIT TO A BLANK CHECK WHICH WOULD DRAMATICALLY EXPAND ALL FEDERAL WELFARE PROGRAMS.

When I commented that I would oppose such a wasteful expansion program, a spokesman for my opponent implied that my position constituted a racial decision. He made the comment that I was just another "good ole boy" who wanted things to be "like they were a hundred years ago."

The issue was one of whether or not huge, wasteful programs should be increased in funding to become larger and more wasteful. Race had absolutely nothing to do with it. Obviously my opponent's side wanted to justify their position by attempting to make it appear to be a racial issue. A classic example of many of the political campaigns in America in which economic issues are used to divide people, not only along economic lines, but also intentionally create dissension between racial groups by stressing economic differences.

We would like to see everyone take the opportunities available in this country to improve their lives and be responsible enough at least to *try* and accomplish something. Ironically, I also think that this means the vast majority of people want people of all races to be successful.

Chapter 2

The Buffet Syndrome — The Full Meal Double-deal

In 2007, after completing the first draft of *The Buffet Syndrome*, I had not yet chosen the title. After a great deal of thought, pondering the many topics I had written about, it struck me that there was one thing in common, whether the topic was people, government bureaucracy, programs, regulatory agencies, loans, food or whatever. The underlying thread was that our country is overrun with people who will take anything they can get as long as someone else pays for it. Thus, *The Buffet Syndrome* was born.

Although this book is about Americans and the Buffet Syndrome, it can also be considered a book about the U.S. government and its people.

I worked on this book for years before finding the missing ingredient, the central theme that would tie all the chapters together: the Buffet Syndrome, which is responsible for America's current plight — a syndrome that has been adopted by a huge portion of the population, and with the constant assistance from a large portion of federal representatives, will head everyone toward the collapse of the system.

It is very important that I clarify something before defining the Buffet Syndrome. I am as sincere in the following statement as is humanly possible. While it might sound like a disclaimer, it certainly is not; it just happens to be the way I believe: The *huge* majority of the people in America are just good people, good citizens of their communities and states — proud of themselves, their jobs, their families, and their country.

Around the world, regardless of the nations involved, the huge majority of people are the same. Whether living in a fully developed nation, a Third World country, or even a nation which has been a problem for the U.S., the majority of people are the same. Even if the U.S. has had serious differences with the leaders of a nation, even been in military conflict at some point, the people are basically good and mean well.

I absolutely will never say that *all* people, under any condition, fit into a certain mold or category, because obviously they do not, and it would be foolish to think that they do. However, as each year goes by, a larger and larger percentage of Americans become involved in the Buffet Syndrome.

So what is it? The Buffet Syndrome is this: TAKING ANYTHING A PERSON CAN GET WITH NO CONSIDERATION WHATSOEVER AS TO THE EFFECTS OF ENGAGING IN SUCH ACTIVITY. In other words, if a person thinks it is available to them, no matter what the situation may be, they will take it. No consideration is given as to what it costs, the effect on anyone else, or the burden on the taxpayers.

To use a simple analogy, visualize a typical buffet restaurant: customers taking plates and getting whatever food they want. A sign reads, "Take a new plate each time you go to the buffet." It's obvious the diners know they can always go back and get whatever additional food they would like to have. Unlike a cafe, where one is very selective when studying the menu, at the buffet *everything* is available.

Think about the number of people who will go into a buffet and make total gluttons of themselves. Knowing full well they can get whatever they want and can stay as long as they want, they will take a plate and, maybe even at the first item that looks good, will throw several pieces on the plate and then stack the plate up with everything else they can *conceivably* eat.

A little while later, there they go again, picking up another plate, taking another run at the buffet, piling on a bunch more stuff, and racing back to the table to see how much they can consume.

Later, an observer may see them with several plates, two or three with more food *left on them* than was consumed. The fact that so much food remains on the table shows they haven't been very selective. But do they care? No, it's a buffet. In their minds they paid one price and it is their right to take everything they want. But they don't stop there.

They go back again, take another plate *to see what they might have missed*. They may have just a little bit of room left in their belly, but it's time to make another run.

Once finished with the main course, or main *courses*, it's time for dessert! Well, do they pick out a single dessert? Never! No telling how many desserts are available, so they take several and head back to their tables. They may be so stuffed that all they can do is pick at one dessert, then another.

They have done about all the damage they could do, taken everything they think they are entitled to, made as big a pig out of themselves as possible, so it's time to leave.

I think of all the times I have sat in that buffet and seen these same people. Keep in mind that it is no small percentage. They made trip after trip after trip. All those plates and all that food left over!

Do they ever consider that people like themselves, wasting food like it was going out of style, must make the cost of the buffet go up for all of the diners? The answer is simple: NO! THEY DON'T CARE.

This is a classic example of what happens when Americans feel like they are *entitled* to something: They think they paid a certain amount for it or they are qualified for it or they discover it is easily available or they are getting it for nothing, so they will take all they can get.

Well, let's go to another buffet just for the heck of it: a pizza buffet. Rather than you and your family ordering a couple of pizzas for delivery to your door, as you so often do, you decide to eat out.

A pizza buffet is really an interesting experiment in human behavior, because some of the people turn into animals, devouring everything in sight. You put everything that you think you could possibly eat on the plate, but you know you can go back in a few minutes, at least for dessert.

I will absolutely guarantee that if you frequent pizza buffets, you will see what I am about to describe. Here comes this person with a plate, perhaps two of them, just stacking slice after slice. Once at his table, he will take a couple of bites off each one, maybe a bite or two from near the center of the slices. There remains half to two-thirds of each slice (the culls) — all discarded. He goes back in a few minutes for more pizza.

It may get even worse. You might look over there in a few minutes to see that he has eaten perhaps a third of each of those pieces, if that. Before he leaves, there may be a few pieces he hasn't even touched or only took one bite of.

Now for dessert! Since there will probably be more than one dessert, and all available for one price, he gets another plate, puts three or four desserts on it, and saves a trip by trying them all at the same time. He may be so stuffed that he can only take a little bite out of each one. Maybe on some he decides he didn't really want them to begin with or he has absolutely no room for them. But what the heck, he paid his good money, so what's the difference?

I remember one buffet I attended (sometimes this is like going to a circus, if the waste wasn't so sad!) where I watched an older couple with a grandson. They gathered in huge plates of pizza, scraped all the toppings into a salad bowl, and just simply ate the toppings! I estimate the three of them rummaged *at least* 50 slices. Not one bite of crust was touched.

Why would anyone do that? Quite simple: It's a classic Buffet Syndrome. In their mind they were entitled; they paid a price, so they are taking it. But what kind of example was that to set for their grandson?

I think you get my point.

At some point in time the restaurant owner or manager will have to control this situation. Like them, our politicians — all of us, really — are going to have to face up to the challenges discussed in the remaining chapters of this book, which are far more horrendous than pizza slices: taking billions of dollars in expenditures that this nation cannot afford. More Americans every year are entering Buffet Syndrome programs that absolutely cost a bundle and get worse every year. We don't want the pizza restaurant to close its doors. We don't want America to become so financially burdened that there is no hope.

Before we leave this chapter, let's go back to my family ordering pizza and staying home. Would we probably order one or two pizzas and eat every slice? Or order six or seven pizzas, eat a third out of the centers, and toss the balance away? Well, we all know the answer. That is the world of difference between Americans being self-supporting and careful not to waste our resources, or giving in to the Buffet Syndrome.

Here's how things have changed in the two restaurants I described in 2007. About three years ago I went back to one of those pizza buffets. There was a group of high school students, all of whom were wearing baseball uniforms from a small town in the Texas Panhandle.

Six players sat at two tables pushed together. Two of the players started what appeared to be a contest. The idea was to see how big a bite could be taken from a slice of pizza and how many slices could be consumed. The whole table, including a man who evidently was the team coach, laughed continuously about what was taking place.

Only one bite was taken from each slice of pizza, so that obviously meant that at least half of each slice was wasted, simply put aside. One of the team members had three large plates of pizza remnants that were stacked very high. I watched him as he proudly counted the remnants on only two of his three plates. There were more than 50 of them. He sure was proud. I took pictures of those two tables after they all left. It was totally disgusting.

About a year ago, I went back to the same pizza restaurant. I had an agreeable visit, because that facility, even though it's a buffet, allows you to order a pizza with whatever toppings you prefer for the standard buffet price. You simply state how large the serving should be in order that your "special" pizza is not wasted. (I never waste food.)

This week, I went back to that same pizza restaurant. Again, you could order your "special" pizza for the standard price, but there was a change. Any topping selected after the first topping would require additional payment, regardless of how small the size of the pizza ordered. The lady said too much special order food got wasted.

Here's what's really sad. Half of the containers at the salad bar area were empty. Only about a third of the pizza buffet area had pans of pizza, so there basically was no selection of anything. I would estimate there were some 40 tables in the facility, and perhaps five of them were occupied by diners. The remaining tables were full of dishes with discarded food. We took the one and only empty table in the entire facility. It was also obvious that not only the floor help was in short supply, but the kitchen help was as well.

The table nearest us was occupied by a man and three young kids. There were numerous plates of food that they never touched. In addition to that, each of the kids had gotten full plates of every dessert item available. They too were never touched. When the four of them walked out the door, I took a look at what was left. It's my guess that what was left over could have fed as many as eight adults. What can I say? All I know is that people couldn't care less. And it is getting worse all over America. In the meantime, the owner or managers of that pizza restaurant still don't recognize, much less deal with, the problem that will eventually cause them to close their doors.

Only two days later, my wife, son and I went to the other pizza restaurant I talked about in 2007. There was an elderly couple sitting at the table next to us. They had a full-sized pizza pan on their table. Here's what we witnessed. They too scraped just the toppings off of the majority of the pizza and ate only those. Nearly all of the slices were left intact.

Before we left that restaurant, both the person cleaning up the area and the cashier were picking up after the diners. I noticed that the cashier commented about the discarded full-size scraped-off slices. Here's what also irritates me. That couple was at least as old as I am. They have certainly been around long enough to witness periods in our history when food just wasn't wasted. This is how far the Buffet Syndrome has progressed.

I wrote extensively in 2007 about how millions of people have become content to live off welfare. Let's talk now about the current status of that acceptance of the welfare life, and has that situation changed?

For the past six years I have traveled to the Rio Grande Valley of Texas to spend the coldest months of the winter. These are some of the things I have witnessed on a regular basis. All of these are examples of how entire families not only accept welfare as a lifestyle, but also plan their everyday lives around it as a goal in life.

I shop a lot at the Walmart store in Alamo, Texas, while in the Valley, just as I shop at the one located in the southwest area of Amarillo, Texas. What happens at those two stores is such a contrast that it's like comparing night and day.

To begin with, at the Amarillo store you rarely see any item that has been taken from its proper display area and moved to some oddball location. You rarely see such things as price tags removed from items and dropped on the floor. You don't see multiple shopping carts packed full with items not purchased at the front checkout stands, which leaves the area so backed up that it's a battle to exit the store once you have checked out. You don't see remnants of packages disposed of, perhaps either partially consumed or completely empty.

Now let's talk about what I see on a regular basis at the location in Alamo. On several occasions, I have seen a family enter the store and immediately head for the area in which take-out foods, including meals and pastry items, were available. It's pretty disgusting to watch an entire family box up one or more packages of pastries. I have seen their kids hollering to mom, dad, or both of them to hurry to that area. I have followed those families as they moved to the next shopping aisle where I witnessed them immediately eating the goodies they had just put into their cart. In other words, the family planned this event as the first stop when doing their shopping.

At the Alamo store, a common sight throughout the entire facility is remnants of items consumed on location. They were in the form of boxes, packages and wrappers with the price tag still on them, along with plenty of small containers, also emptied.

The last time I went to the Alamo store just before I returned to Amarillo this year, I saw a man with two boys around the ages of 6 and 8. As soon as they entered the store, they made a quick run to the fruit and vegetable area. The boys were obviously excited and the dad had a big smile on his face. A large bag of grapes was selected and placed in the rear part of the shopping cart. As soon as they got around the corner all three dug in. I did a bit more shopping and kept an eye on that group periodically. By the time they got to the rear of the store, the bag of grapes was empty. I also noticed earlier that a few more items had been placed in the basket, such as cookies. Those items were no longer in the shopping cart.

I have gotten to the point that while waiting in line to check out, I predict (quietly to my wife) what will likely transpire with some of the shoppers ahead of us. It's easy to guess how those shoppers will pay for what is in their shopping carts. There are four forms of payment — cash, Lone Star cards, credit cards, and W.I.C. (Women, Infants and Children) cards. In addition to that, the use of the Lone Star card creates a common "disposal" activity that is almost unbelievable. (The Lone Star card is the food stamp program in Texas.)

A lot of shoppers divide their items in the shopping cart into three distinct sections. They also plan on mainly using each of the following three forms of payment to the maximum extent possible — Lone Star card, W.I.C. card and cash. The W.I.C. card is used for very basic items such as milk, cheese, and cereal. The Lone Star card is used for everything else, based upon the decision to either accept or reject items as food. This decision is made either by the checkout employee or the management at various stores.

It goes something like this: The first type of purchase

will be with the Lone Star card. It's very common to see a shopper attempt to purchase not only food, but additional items that are not even close to being food. I have seen items literally tossed to the next aisle, dropped on the floor or even thrown over the shoulder by customers that never had the slightest intention of paying cash for such things as toys and clothing, if they are rejected by Lone Star.

The checkout areas are a mess due to the discarded items. Customers then use their cash or credit cards, and then the W.I.C cards. You would not believe how many items these people picked up in one area of the store and then disposed of on the shelves in another area. That's even before they enter the checkout area with the items they will only purchase if one of their cards approves them.

While standing in line to check out I have stood behind plenty of people who set numerous items to the side. Like all the items moved around throughout the store, this shows that a lot of people have absolutely no regard whatsoever for the property of others. A common sight are perishable items, such as steaks or frozen foods, simply stacked on a shelf somewhere.

One last story to put this into perspective. Last year while in the Valley, a young lady was checking out just ahead of me. She was young, probably in her late 20s. She was dressed in beautiful clothing and I would describe her as looking like a professional model. She used the Lone Star card, W.I.C. card, and cash for her purchases. What was unusual though, was that she bought most of her groceries using the Lone Star card, four gallons of milk using the W.I.C. card, and cash for her remaining items, while the back of her cart was totally full of cosmetics. I would estimate there were at least 20 different cosmetic items and the total cash price was more than $200. There's something wrong with this picture.

All of these examples bring to mind a question we need to ask ourselves: Since the entire family is playing the game, it's a planned event, and there's no respect for anyone they are dealing with, so what are the chances that entitlement programs will ever be brought under control?

Chapter 3

The Good Times Never End

Americans are being indoctrinated into believing that if a person can do or buy something today, that's all that matters, that there are no consequences associated with immediate gratification. This message goes out to all Americans.

We are encouraged to spend money and virtually ignore long-term financial obligations. We have a marketing oriented society, and it is very successful. That's the free enterprise system, part of our capitalist system, and it's fine for it to be that way. That's the way it was intended to be.

But Americans market products and services of every conceivable nature to prospective clients from every conceivable part of society. We are constantly inundated through the various media to purchase the products, services, ideas, or even political views of anyone who believes that many of us are totally naive.

So how is the economic health of America measured? Let's say a TV announcer states that, according to the latest figures, the economy is strong. Well, what is his *basis* in saying that the economy is strong?

Please keep in mind that we have plenty of economic experts who can summarize all the many factors which affect the economy. They can correlate the indexes, inflation, interest rates, various reports, historical trends, political decisions, world trade imbalances, debts, or what have you. In other words, there is no end to the amount of information that can be accumulated to clarify or confuse the issue. There is no shortage of factors that affect America's economy, and there is no shortage of so-called experts to further confuse us in answering the question.

Quite often reporters say that unemployment is low or that inflation is low. Here is the main reason, though, for saying the economy is good: CONSUMER SPENDING IS UP.

Even those same financial analysts, who can cite hundreds of reasons why the economy is either good or bad, or will be good or bad if we follow their analysis, still come back to that same big issue. If consumer spending is high, the times are good. If consumer spending decreases, the economy is not doing so hot.

On the surface, making an increase in consumer spending the main barometer for measuring the economic health of America might sound good. But if one looks below the surface, it is simply a sign of a nation that is fooling itself.

In order to really measure how good or how bad the economy is, other important factors must be considered. One needs to consider inflation, long- and short-term debt, the huge trade deficit, the unfortunate fact that we have become a service economy, the lack of personal savings, and the loss of American jobs to other countries, especially in industry and manufacturing. Then consider the total tax liability to the nation and the role of government programs.

Consumer spending is totally out of control for many millions of Americans, who are in debt up to their eyeballs and can't even understand why. I wish I could say out-of-control debt affects only a relatively few families. But the truth is that it is a way of life for millions of Americans and now seems to be an accepted philosophy of how to live in this country.

Whether by paying cash or taking on a financial obligation, millions of Americans buy everything they want, as long as they can find a way to purchase it. In other words, if there's a way they can have it today, then to hell with tomorrow.

If there is one thing America is *not,* it's a saving nation. According to the latest report I heard a few months ago, the average savings per family is 7/10 of 1 percent *below* zero. There is no question that many Americans put plenty of money into accounts that are not traditional savings accounts, and that is understandable. A savings account at a typical bank offers only a minimal return, considering the very low interest rate paid.

In addition, those savings are fully taxable, and of course inflation is also a factor. It's only natural that low interest-bearing savings accounts, fully taxable and subject to inflationary pressures, are not a desirable investment alternative to many people in the "middle class."

People put money into retirement accounts, such as IRAs and company retirement programs, along with many other investment vehicles including stocks, bonds, real estate, etc. Here's where the savings problem in America exists. There are many millions of families in America that live payday to payday and have no savings, retirement, or equity in anything.

There are millions of people currently living only on Social Security, along with any other tax funded assistance programs for which they might qualify. There are many millions more who are approaching retirement age who will also be totally dependent on government programs for the rest of their lives. There is a train wreck coming that cannot be avoided, and it will be massive in scope.

Despite all warnings, Americans continue to spend, with more than $8,000 in credit card debt for the average family. We are not talking about a tiny percentage of families. Over $8,000 is the average of *all* American families.

How did so many millions of Americans get themselves into this situation? To me, a large percentage of families are so totally undisciplined in their financial lives that, when faced with huge debts and monthly payments in which perhaps only the interest is being paid each month, they simply buy more things they don't need and can't afford.

I have seen examples during the past couple of years of just how undisciplined people can be. In both cases I'm about to relate, I even attempted to help them financially to get out of the traps they were in.

One person had many talents in the building and construction business. When faced with plenty of bills, very little income, limited transportation, and existence in a cracker-box house, he was given everything needed to start a very profitable business. Rather than seizing the opportunity of a lifetime, he chose to sleep late every morning, goof off all afternoon, and spend the money designated for operating the business on a wasteful hobby. Some people are content to barely scrape by, avoiding responsibility, take something for nothing, and all the while look for a welfare program to sign up for.

Another example was a person who had absolutely nothing and had been waiting for economic assistance from a federal agency. I helped the person get that assistance. The check finally came in, covering a lengthy prior period of time, and was put to immediate use. However, more than half of that one-time distribution was spent on a newly-purchased car and a significant part of the remainder was used to purchase a computer system. Today, that person has what he started with — absolutely nothing.

Many Americans shop credit card companies, changing companies to get more available cash to pay on already delinquent accounts, or perhaps look for introductory rates that last only a few months. That just gets them into more trouble and the situation simply worsens. They may eventually get some idea what is happening, but in the meantime, they have done exactly what the marketers suggest and our financial experts praise as being the main attribute of a strong economy. They bought more stuff and their consumer status has increased.

Millions of families live from payday to payday, driving the best vehicle they can make payments on and living in the best home they were able to afford. Again, I am talking about a huge number of people. They drive vehicles with payments that might last 72 months and live in houses they "bought" with payments that will last 30 years.

The irony in this situation is that the vehicle was probably priced beyond their means when purchased, and therefore is probably not worth what is owed on it at almost any point in the payoff. As to the house they moved into, there is a strong possibility they won't develop any equity in it because they will probably take equity out of their home by borrowing against it to raise cash.

Starting about five years ago, home financing took on a really strange modification. Although 25- and 30-year mortgages have been commonplace for decades, and variable interest rate mortgages have been around for many years, what is relatively new is *truly* creative lending for home mortgages. These creative programs allow more people to accomplish what has been considered the American Dream for decades, owning a home. But at a big price.

To follow up with the 2007 discussion of "creative financing," I would remind you that following the bust of 2008, we heard that plenty of Americans wound up with no equity in their homes, many owing perhaps twice as much as the homes were valued. That didn't surprise me at all. The question is: How did they wind up in such a position?

In a nutshell, here is what it all boiled down to: Institutions were pressured into making home loans to many unqualified potential home purchasers by threats from our federal government. Those loans — tens of thousands of them — violated every acceptable sound business practice, and we all know how that turned out.

There is one factor though that made this housing fiasco even worse. For many decades there have been credit ratings for loans based upon the collateral which helps guarantee the credibility of the loan. Real estate, such as homes – which are collateral for loans – had almost universally been considered mortgage-backed securities. Most of that portfolio of homes would be rated triple A.

In short, the government passed legislation that pressured lending institutions to give unqualified people an opportunity to get home loans outside normal business guidelines. Lending institutions believed the legislation from the House and Senate practically promised that the government was guaranteeing these loans — not true. However, the loans were made to the world.

The newest creative home lending program is called home equity loans. Let me tell a little story to demonstrate the catastrophic effects.

I recently had my secretary contact one of these home equity loan companies to send me their package about getting a loan. I would like to relate some of the parts of that package.

But first, please understand that a home equity loan is designed to get cash out of a home that is currently owned, rather than purchase a home. In a normal home loan, a family attempts to qualify for a loan to purchase a home and there are many prerequisites for qualification. The equity loan is very different.

Let's say that hypothetically, rather than trying to get cash out of a house for whatever reason, the same rationale of the home equity loan company was to be used to initially purchase the home. Would equity loan parameters mirror acceptable business practices? No way.

It is important to also note that "creative financing" is very common in America — involving up to 75 percent of home purchases, according to latest reports. Even worse though, in 60 percent of all mortgages the payments are interest only for the first several years. In other words, those so-called homeowners are developing no equity whatsoever in their homes. Creative financing can also consist of such things as dual mortgages (a first and a second mortgage), a low down payment far below traditional standards, and perhaps an overly optimistic calculation of the borrower's income.

I was surprised to see what was presented in the package. Here are some of the ways a person can get into one of these home equity loans: no down payment, no closing costs whatsoever, or perhaps make interest payments only.

"How much do you have to put down?" is no longer a serious issue. I recall the days when it was commonplace to put 5 to 10 percent down on a home. If a person did not have the money, he had to borrow from family, friends, or a bank. He simply had to have it, save to get it, or at least make some reasonable down payment.

Well, under these new programs, how about 1 percent down or perhaps $500, whichever is the lesser amount?

In the old days, a person had to have good credit and a good employment record. How about now? What if a person has no credit at all? The loan companies don't even run a credit check. They might say they will, but they won't verify it.

How about instead of having one mortgage, a person has two mortgages? How is he going to pay for both houses? They don't seem concerned.

What if he can't even show earnings from any source? Or if he can show earnings, are they verified? Probably not. How about his employment? He has to have some way to pay for the house. They may not even check to see if he has a job!

After all these "provisions" are met, and there is not much to look at, where will a person end up after getting one of these loans? Well, he and his family are able to pay off some bills. But they were in debt and they are still in debt. They may get out of the current mess on a temporary basis, but they are also stuck with a larger, newer mortgage. And there is a strong possibility that part of that home equity money will be used to purchase more stuff they could live without.

On the positive side, which is slim at best, if he one day loses the house, he didn't have a fortune invested.

So do they really have equity now, on a house they probably couldn't afford? No. They simply have more debt.

These creative mortgages have an adverse effect on the real estate market in America. One serious impact is that a person may buy the most expensive house he can, pay a premium for it, and thereby distort the true values of homes in the area. If he can move into a house (basically with no qualifications at all and no money at risk) appraised at, say, $115,000, creative financing raised the cost of the house to about $125,000. And since tax agencies equate worth to what someone will pay to get a house, then that house is now appraised at $125,000. Well, what about similar houses in the neighborhood? They must be worth more, too. So the taxes go up on them and we find homeowners suddenly burdened by tax increases on homes which have been "improved" by nothing more than proximity to an overpriced home.

I recently went to a foreclosure sale near my hometown of Amarillo, Texas. I saw foreclosure after foreclosure. When I looked at the houses that were offered and the amounts of money that was owed on those houses, for all practical purposes the owners had no equity. The buyers must have been engaging in creative financing of some sort — the value simply wasn't there. It's kind of like that car that will take 72 months to pay for. At any time, it simply is not worth what is owed against it.

And when a large mortgage and other debts consume a couple's dollars, the future becomes precarious. What happens when a typical husband and wife, both of whom work full-time, encounter an unexpected financial problem? What if one of them loses their job? What if a new baby comes along? What happens if there is a serious illness or long-term disability? Since 100 percent of their combined income is committed to maintaining their current lifestyle and paying toward indebtedness, missing only one paycheck will cause consternation to the family. But if a major interruption of their usual income occurs, disaster may follow. The family has no savings, owes more on their car than it is worth, has no equity in their house, has been paying only the necessary minimum on their credit cards, and now faces a financial crisis.

The entire world knows that in 2008 the housing disaster took place. That event wasn't confined to just a few states, a few mortgage companies, a few banks, a few governmental entities or for that matter, even a few nations.

It appeared that the housing bust came from out of nowhere to the total surprise of virtually everyone, affecting millions of homeowners, basically destroying financial institutions, having a significant effect on national elections, and dividing our nation even more.

For whatever it might be worth, the housing bust came as no surprise to me. I knew it was coming and had written about the home financing mess in 2007. I knew what caused the problem, how it would play out, who would take the blame for it and just how big the bust would be. It was my belief in the autumn of 2007, the crash was already overdue to take place.

The one thing I didn't expect was how vile politicians would get in their attempts to shift the blame to anyone other than themselves.

In 2007 I wrote extensively about home financing, all the various games being played to get home loans, and so on. What I did not talk about was what led up to the tossing aside of common sense and sound business practices.

The politics that caused the entire mess to begin with had taken place several years prior by federal legislation that insured the demise of the housing industry. That legislation evolved from both the United States House of

Representatives and the United States Senate. Specifically, it came from the House Budget Committee and the Senate Finance Committee. The two men who spearheaded that disastrous piece of legislation were Congressmen Barney Frank and Chris Dodd.

The nature of the bill was that anyone in America should qualify to own a home. The bill was enacted to insure that people of limited financial means and persons of all ethnic backgrounds would be placed in the position of achieving the American dream, that of home ownership. It put lending institutions into a strange predicament. They received many applications for home loans that, if granted, would exceed sound lending/business practices. Yet most were approved.

You must keep in mind that it was a common sight to see demonstrators in front of financial institutions demanding that home mortgages be approved. All that was before the bust in 2008, and even before the autumn of 2007.

Sadly, this scenario is not infrequent. Yet, the economy is deemed to be healthy because money continues to be spent. For too many, the myth that the good times never end eventually shatters their American Dream.

Chapter 4

The Federal Bureaucracy

What is bureaucracy? Let's consider the bureau in your bedroom. There is a chest of drawers, stacked top to bottom, and probably a mirror on top. The drawers are all part of the same bureau, but there are no connections between them, each is separate. One drawer at my house has my socks, another my underwear, another some letters I need to save, and the bottom drawers contain miscellaneous items that I don't know what to do with but may need someday.

A government agency is often called a bureau. It is usually comprised of departments, all consigned to different tasks, probably existing without much internal communication. Each of the departments may consider itself a "top drawer." Any reflection made by the bureau to the outer world is generally a desire for permanence more than a statement of true relevance or a guarantee of quality in past performance.

A bureaucracy is characterized by separate departments functioning in rigid, autocratic routines. The major purpose of the agency is often reduced to routine, red tape, and turf wars. In the struggle of each department to reach the top of the bureaucratic hierarchy, the reasons for the very existence of the department, and perhaps the agency itself, may be altered, ignored, or even totally forgotten.

And a person who functions perfectly in a bureaucracy is, of course, a bureaucrat. Mr. Webster's dictionary tells us that a bureaucrat is prone to work "in a fixed routine without exercising intelligent judgment" (*Webster's Universal College Dictionary,* 1997).

Now, when Congress passes a bill to create an agency to deal with a perceived problem, it also specifies a notification process so citizens who are benefited by the new legislation can be made aware of it. I believe that this mandated process actually *solicits participation* at the local level. It is the law that people must not only be told that the new program exists, but also how they might prosper from it and how to qualify for it.

Because the Buffet Syndrome is rampant, many people will say, "Hey, somebody is going to get something. I don't want to be left out, so I'd better go sign up!"

Congress is using the Buffet Syndrome to verify the importance of their legislation and their jobs. By catering to certain groups, by controlling public funding to specific areas, votes can be swayed. So Congress is utilizing everything available to them to maintain incumbency, whether all these programs are necessary or not. They too are dining at the Taxpayers' Buffet.

This seditious practice solicits participation by people who may be only marginally qualified. Even if they never get a check, it's something for nothing — well, almost nothing: make a phone call, fill out some forms, but no real labor. Even if they don't *need* the money, they may rationalize, "If I'm entitled to it, I want it." To be quite honest, in most situations people simply don't care. The Buffet Syndrome strikes again.

The bureaucracy absolutely must spend its budget, or suffer a budget cut in the next session. Consequently, a bureaucracy will always spend its budget, right down to the last nickel, if it can. Then they can tell Congress, "We were under funded and utilized our entire budget." When the next budget talks start, they will be looking for an increase.

Now, on the positive side, it is very important to note that not all agencies waste money by overstaffing administration. Many agencies are extremely efficient and do a great job. They carry out the intent of the law and service their communities well.

Also, many employees in various agencies work very hard doing *necessary* functions. They take a lot of pride in their work, serve the public admirably, and are dedicated to doing a good job, just like people in private industry. The fact that they happen to be working in a state, federal, or local tax supported entity is immaterial.

Yet some agencies simply become a bureaucratic waste of taxpayers' money. They get so totally out of control that they have no legitimate function. Administrative costs become prohibitive because they utilize the budget for payroll expansion and empire building, robbing funds from the intended recipients of the program.

I define "empire building" as the policy of hiring more and more people to fill more and more unnecessary jobs, which expand the agency yet create stumbling blocks and increase inefficiency.

The rationale to an agency executive is to develop authority over more people and receive a higher income by supposedly being in a more responsible position. By having more people in his or her empire, that position can be ranked higher and the empire builder can be paid more.

It is not uncommon for hard-working, dedicated employees to become totally disenchanted with their empire-building bosses and the unnecessary supervisors who serve little or no function within the agency.

Too often, the worst bureaucracies, those most guilty of empire building and deviation from the stated objective of the agency, and the biggest purveyors of red tape and obfuscation, belong to the federal government.

Federal bureaucracy isn't just located in Washington. National headquarters is usually there, but an agency's offices may be located in any state, any community, including small towns. A local office of a bloated federal agency, in all probability, will be as inefficient, overstaffed, and out of touch with the people as its headquarters.

One of the basic truths of government is this: The closer

the headquarters of any tax supported office is to the taxpayer, the more likely it will serve the public in an efficient manner. In other words, city and county offices are generally very efficient. State offices are more removed from the people. Sometimes it is difficult to determine where the funding comes from for certain state offices. In those cases a person will probably deal with added bureaucracy.

One reason why the federal system is totally out of control is that money can only be manufactured at the federal level. That reality puts cities, counties, and states in their proper places, in the view of the federal bureaucracy, who has the power, and uses it.

Only at the federal level can a congressman or senator author a spending bill that makes him look like a hero in his district, yet is paid for by taxpayers across the country.

It is also at the federal level that mandated programs can be created which demand that funding be supplied by state or even local government — county or city. Quite often, substantial local tax funds must be used to administer federally mandated programs.

I now want to cite some firsthand examples of events that can happen in agencies, truly classic situations I have encountered over the years. Further proof of my firsthand knowledge can be found in the About the Author and the Publisher section at the back of the book.

While running for Congress in the 1980s, I spent almost a full week meeting with various agencies of the Department of Agriculture. One of my meetings was with the head of the Foreign Agricultural Service. Two outer offices had been designated for secretaries to aid that illustrious person. As I waited, I noticed that one of the two secretaries was spending the entire time on a personal phone call that she was obviously enjoying.

I watched the second secretary in her office. She put a piece of paper in her typewriter, moved the carriage back and forth several times, making sure it was nice and straight before typing. Using one finger on each hand, very slowly, she managed to complete one line. She rolled the paper out of the typewriter and held it up to examine her work.

Once she was certain that the page looked real good, she folded it lengthwise, running her finger down the edge, front and back, assuring the fold to be perfect. Confident that it was, she dropped the sheet carefully in the wastebasket and started another, time after time after time.

After a delay of about an hour, my meeting began, with five people present. I was there primarily to inquire about agriculture programs in various nations of the world. I wanted information on crop yields and whether or not certain agriculture programs were in place in those respective governments, such as outlays to farmers for crop subsidies, crop insurance, subsidies for transportation of the harvests to markets, etc.

After being in a roundtable discussion for some 15 to 20 minutes and not getting any meaningful answers to my questions, the director sensed my frustration and turned to a lady, asking her about a study that recently had been completed and would probably contain answers to many of my questions.

The lady was, evidentially, a ranking staff person in another division at the Department of Agriculture. She had contracted a private company to supply a great deal of data.

She asked to be excused for a few minutes to go back to her office, which appeared to be some distance from the office we were meeting in. The Agriculture Department's office building is huge.

When she returned, she brought the *original* survey, done by a consulting firm that had polled countries all over the world. Date stamped, it had been received approximately six weeks prior.

This was a very expensive survey for taxpayers to pay for, but here is the most amazing part of the story: When that survey was finished, after consultants had traveled around the world to many nations to get all that information, she had taken the report and put it in her desk drawer. It was never copied, discussed, offered to anybody, or evidently, even read.

I want to give you some examples of bureaucracy at the state level. Years ago I worked for the State of Texas in an agency which oversees tax collections. First, we had a strange work routine. We had to be in the office between 8:00 and 9:00 a.m.; usually out visiting businesses in the middle of the day, but not contacting anyone between 11:00 a.m. and 1:00 p.m.; and then back in the office from 4:00 to 5:00.

My position was known as Taxpayer Compliance Officer. In a nutshell, I and several other TCOs were field agents employed by the Texas Comptroller of Public Accounts. The group of agents/TCOs worked in the top 26 counties of Texas, that being the Texas Panhandle, and our duties on many days were primarily outside the district office in Amarillo. At least that was what it was *supposed* to be.

The group of us had to operate under a crazy set of guidelines. The main thing I did each day was fill out the report on what I did that day. It was impossible to do a reasonable amount of work during any day, considering a late start from the district office, hiding out for at least two hours around the noon hour, and then making certain I was physically present in the office an hour before quitting time.

The report I filled out each day was very detailed and included where I had gone, who I had contacted, for what reason, the mileage (if outside of Amarillo), and the length of time for each stop. The state also had a formula that instructed me to never show less than some minimum period of time for each contact, whether I used that time or not.

The daily time sheet took more time to complete than almost any task encountered on any day. Due to the procedures established, such as timeframes to meet and minimum times to be shown, it was impossible to do an honest day's work. The only real task to complete on a daily basis was to prepare that bureaucratic time sheet, which forced everybody to be an outright liar, and not by their own choice.

My immediate supervisor called me in one day and said, "Ron, what are you tryin' to do?"

I said, "I don't have any idea what you're talking about."

"I'm talkin' about your daily report."

I reminded him that I could only do so much in a day because I had to be in the office between 8:00 and 9:00 a.m., I couldn't call anyone between 11:00 and 1:00, and I had to be in the office between 4:00 and 5:00. That didn't give me a lot of time to do what I was supposed to be doing.

He kept on talking.

I was growing a bit confused. Then it dawned on me. His complaint was that I was doing too much work! I was messing up the system! I needed to show less activity on my time sheets because I was making the other employees look bad.

I thought to myself, "This is idiotic, to be called on the carpet for doing too much work!" I wondered how much more productive I would be without that crazy time sheet, and how much more trouble I would be in!

While employed at that same bureaucratic agency, another example of inefficiency popped up. Amarillo is in about the middle of the Panhandle. I was in Pampa, about an hour northeast. A little town 23 miles east-northeast of there is called Miami, which could have been my next stop. But I had to go see a guy who had a business located a few miles north of Pampa, so I went there, then east, right into Miami.

My expense report was delayed for about a week and I got called in by my supervisor again. He said, "What are you doin'?"

I said, "What do you mean?"

"You can't go from a city to someplace and then go to another city."

"Well, why not?"

He carefully explained the rule. "You have to go from the city to wherever you are going, back to that same city and then go city to city."

"Look, that's extra miles I didn't drive, shouldn't be paid

for, and am not entitled to."

"You can't do that."

"That's strange, because I just did."

To me, the rule was totally crazy, and my opinion has not been tempered by the years.

The big boss of this particular organization came to Amarillo from Austin. He was over all of the field offices, but I learned that he had come to Amarillo just to see me. That didn't help my nerves any as I shut the door to the office he had borrowed for our conversation.

He came right to the point. He said someone overheard me say that I was not going to vote for a certain state official.

I said, "No, I'm not."

"Well, are you going to vote for the opposition party?"

"No. I'm not going to have to because this guy is going to get beat in the primary election."

He wasn't very happy. Then he let me leave.

I still had my job, but thought it was amazing that he may have come all the way from Austin just to see me because he overhead I wasn't going to vote for his political friend. What a waste of taxpayers' money.

I soon began to look for a better job, to leave the most disgusting job of my entire life! I was led, by Providence or luck, into the oil and gas business, which I have remained in, to at least some degree, to this day.

Occasionally I find myself in Yankton, South Dakota, in an office there, due to my oil connections. Yankton is located immediately down-river about four miles from the last dam on the Missouri River, the Gavins Point Dam, which creates the Lewis and Clark Reservoir. The hydroelectric dam has been releasing a lot of water for a long time, but for a period of time it was not releasing as much water as usual, and a little temporary sandbar appeared out in the riverbed. A few small Piping Plover birds made their nests there. When it was time to start releasing water at usual levels, somebody said that the dam operators could not destroy the habitat of the Piping Plover birds. The fact that the birds had been living nicely for years in that area without the temporary sandbar did not matter.

The decision to protect the birds created a serious problem 65 miles downstream at Sioux City, Iowa, and points south. Barges are relied upon to move agricultural products from those highly productive areas all the way to the mouth of the Mississippi. But barges need water, and when they ground to a halt, other, more expensive means had to be found. When prices dramatically increased and barge employees suffered, government representatives and agencies were contacted, naturally.

To make matters even more complicated, several national agencies tried to exercise authority over each another. Also, agencies of two states, South Dakota and Nebraska, entered the fray — soon followed by the U.S. Corps of Engineers.

While the battle raged, one federal agency even hired a barge and a work crew to build up the sandbar to create an even better artificial habitat. But at some point human suffering was too great (or the Gavins Point Dam was about to burst), water was allowed to flow once again, the temporary sandbar washed away, and all was back to normal. Yet at what cost, in lost productivity in the barge industry and tax dollars?

Approximately 10 years ago I sent a land rights document out of my office to Harris County, Texas, to have it recorded. Harris County is in Houston, the fourth largest city in the U.S. The document was only a few pages and I enclosed the usual check for $12.00. I got a letter back a week or so later with the document unrecorded. A lady had written a full-page letter, explaining that the fee had increased to $13.00, how she had discussed the $1.00 shortfall with her immediate supervisor and another person in a supervisory position, and that the decision coming out of their meeting was that I had to pay the additional $1.00 before it could be recorded.

The question is this: Why not send it back recorded and tell me I owe $1.00? It's pretty bad when a person is able to discuss the issue with at least two supervisors, have a meeting to determine that I still owed $1.00, write a personal letter, then pay the postage to send it back unrecorded. This incident suggests that there were too many people working in that office, wasting taxpayers' money.

I guess over the past 10 years things haven't changed much, or they have gotten worse. I had another document to file and wanted to be certain that my check for the filing fee would be in the correct amount. I had my secretary call that Harris County Office to confirm what the filing fee would be.

When told the amount was to be $28.00, the document and check were mailed to Houston. A few days later I got a letter. The document and my $28.00 check were returned to me, with a letter stating the proper charge was only $24.00. Also included was a form explaining five different filing fees.

My question is this: Why didn't they just file the document and send it back to me along with their check for $4.00? Why mail it back to me — which of course means the cost to Harris County is more — plus unnecessary additional handling for both of us?

They finally mailed the recorded document to me. A few days later another letter arrived, containing a cash register receipt for my $24.00. The question is this: Why couldn't all of the items, my recorded document, their check which could have been issued for my $4.00 overpayment, and the cash register receipt, have been done in one mailing from them, rather than three, which means I would have done a single mailing rather than two?

The reason is simple: That office is obviously overstaffed, inefficient, and a classic bureaucracy at the state level. I should also mention that very large cities begin to mirror federal bureaucracies, which in many cases are overstaffed and inefficient.

While I am on this subject, I would like give a couple of examples from offices in other states that involve county clerk or recorders' offices. I wouldn't want my Texas friends to think I am only picking on them!

During the past year or so, my office has forwarded many

documents for recording. In each case my secretary called that specific office, explained the document to be filed, number of pages, and other requirements in order to get the recording fee. You would not believe the number of times documents were returned unfiled because the fee *stated over the phone* was not correct. What I have found is that there are several states that employ clerks who are either totally incompetent or wake up in a new world every day.

Outside this mayhem is Oklahoma. I don't know what Oklahoma is doing to increase efficiency in their state and county offices, but it is working. They operate tax-supported offices as if they were customer-oriented private businesses. It's no wonder that people in the oil and gas business like working in Oklahoma, where tax-supported entities all across the state provide a refreshing experience: quality employees and supervisors with ability and common sense doing their very best in carrying out duties on behalf of the public.

On a local level, has the reader ever noticed how some public buildings that house tax-supported offices grow in size? Perhaps a school administration office which has been in the same building for many years suddenly moves into a massive building. Why? The town has not quadrupled in population, so why the big building?

Now, in defense of expansion is this: With many federal mandates being handed down to local entities, forcing them to administer and carry out bureaucratic programs, they have to expand. And their tax paying and fee-paying neighbors have to support an out-of-control federal bureaucracy, while on the surface everything looks local.

However, practically every local government in America invites trouble due to their own Buffet Syndrome. Locally elected leaders make it a standard practice to get every possible dollar from the federal government. There is a virtual clearinghouse of information available about programs and funds for which they might qualify; thus, Washington gains even more control over local communities.

As in the case of the individuals at the pizza parlor, the

consensus is, "If we don't get it, some other city will." So billions of dollars each year in so-called federal funding are spread across the nation, in most cases, for questionable needs.

It is commonplace to attempt to fabricate, create, or justify a "need" for the funding just because it is available. In the meantime, there might be some real needs in that community that can't be dealt with, due to a lack of local funding.

This practice gets worse every year. Local governments, as well as individuals caving in to the out-of-control national bureaucracy, simply create more out-of-control bureaucracy on every level.

Do you recall the days before computers when the only ways to correspond were through the mail, by telephone, or perhaps Western Union? Remember standing in a long line, watching the postal clerks perform their duties? You undoubtedly saw many postal clerks greet you at their positions with a smile and sincere desire to help you in your mailing needs. Perhaps it was like going into a corner market and dealing with your friends and neighbors. It would be wonderful if postal patrons, especially the business community, looked forward to going to their postal facility several times each week and dealing with their friends, the postal clerks. And most clerks are trying to do their best.

Unfortunately, significant differences often exist in personnel performing the same work duties. Think about those times in which you stood in line and observed a clerk moving so slowly that you thought he might be a big wind-up toy, and any second he would stop completely. Did you get a smile and a warm greeting when stepping up to his position, or perhaps just a sneer or frown, as though you were an annoyance to his routine? In reality, he is just a low-level bureaucrat who is a bottleneck to commerce. I have discovered that an extremely small percentage of the clerks don't want to deal with the public but have bid on the clerk's position since it offers more favorable work hours. And the union protects them. They are fallbacks to the pre-computer days, when many bureaucrats, high and low, realized they had captive customers and acted accordingly.

It's also understandable how many employees working within the bureaucracy can become totally disgusted with their work environment and their bureaucratic supervisors.

Let me tell you a story that I have been very close to for many years, where I have made an attempt to bring some sanity to a disgusting situation. It involves employees, bureaucratic bungling, the public, and the United States Postal Service.

For more than 20 years, every business day when I was in town, I opened my box and attended to other chores at a post office on West 45th Street. With four clerks servicing my zip code, 79109, I almost never had to wait in line more than a few moments before being able to walk up to one of them.

Not that many years ago, the post office was closed and replaced with one some six blocks away, the Lone Star Station. Unfortunately, it is the center for two additional zip codes, 79110 and 79118. The new post office is massive in size, with dozens of delivery vehicles operating from its back doors. It is also a distribution center.

I went from a facility that was serving the public quite well to a new facility that has never been designed to service the public in a customer-friendly manner. Although there has been a huge increase in the number of people coming to the new facility, there has been a decrease in the number of clerks available to service these customers, from the previous four stations to three.

And, believe it or not, only on rare occasions are all three positions open — usually only one! I have stood in line 20 to 30 minutes plenty of times. People by the hundreds have stood in line for extended periods of time before giving up and leaving. Bear in mind, this isn't something that happens from time to time. It's every day.

Some three years ago I was fed up with that post office mess. I was operating a radio station and we started running "announcements" on the air about the deplorable situation at the Lone Star Station.

Well, maybe we helped. Because of pressure placed upon the post office to do something, an additional service desk was opened in the lobby across from the clerks' stations. At least people could buy stamps there and do some of their tasks, reducing the long wait time.

You might like to know that the new service desk has not been staffed for many months now, so it may as well not even exist. The Lone Star Station is a typical example of bureaucracy in action, or inaction. It was never well designed for customer service, and seldom fully staffed. They couldn't care less how long someone has to stand in line for "service," and they have no plans to deal with reality. In other words, to hell with postal customers, who are a relatively captive consumer base.

It's not the clerks. It's the bureaucratic management that protects itself while having absolutely no regard for either the employees that have to deal with a very upset public, or the public itself. I would describe the Lone Star Station as a total disaster.

It really gives you a warm feeling knowing how you rate as a customer, doesn't it? Think about that when you and countless others are standing in line for 20 to 30 minutes, waiting on one clerk.

The other day, as I was standing in that line for the millionth time, I did some calculations. If 10 people wait for only 10 minutes each, 10 times during a given week, that's some 16 hours of time lost by very busy people. This does not include those who might have stood in line a few minutes before giving up, or those who made a special trip to the post office and turned around once they saw a long line.

But reality is far worse. On most days, nearly the entire day, every customer has to wait 15 to 20 minutes. With only 10 people waiting in line for 15 minutes each during two-thirds of the day, that's a total of 3,600 minutes, or 60 hours of potentially productive time!

Right then I decided that the next day I would put the post office to a test, put them on the clock, quite literally.

On Wednesday, September 5, 2007, I entered the Lone Star Station. I started in the waiting line at 12:43 p.m., the 12th person in line. Only one postal clerk was present. The facility across the lobby from the clerk's stations was closed, as expected. As I waited, several people rang the buzzer by the door that leads to the main part of the building; they needed to pick up certified mail or packages. But nobody ever came out to help them. One lady remarked that she had waited at least half an hour yesterday to pick up an item, only to give up and leave. She gave up again.

Many people came into the facility and waited, then finally gave up and left. One man remarked to me that he had, in the past, waited for as much as an hour trying to get service. He gave up again today.

At 1:08 p.m. a second clerk came to one of the vacant stations. At 1:10 p.m., after standing in line for 27 minutes, I made it. When I completed my business there I counted those still waiting: 21 now. I said to them, and anyone else who cared to listen, "For the information of the 21 of you waiting in line, the story about this fiasco will be included in a book to be published this year. This place is a disgrace." I walked out the door.

My little test was very scientific. I had plenty of witnesses on hand when it took place. And it, unfortunately, is easily repeatable.

No, the problems associated with this facility are not caused by the clerks at their stations. I would hate to have a job where everybody you come in contact with is mad, disgusted, or in a hurry to make up for lost time. Approximately two-and-a-half years ago I called the U.S. Postal Service Office which supervises the Amarillo facilities. I told the lady of the almost daily trials in which I, and many others, had to stand in lengthy lines. Her response was truly breathtaking; she corrected me, saying that nobody ever had to stand in line more than five minutes!

I wonder what hundreds of patrons would say about that, those who have had to put up with this intolerable situation many, many times over many years! I took her comments to mean that I'm a liar, or that she did not want to accept reality. One thing for sure, she, along with the local management of the facility, couldn't care less what the public thinks. Doesn't it make you feel good to know that a local postal facility manager can get incentive pay at the expense of a decent work environment for his employees, all the while thumbing his nose at the customers coming to his facility?

I have found out something very interesting about the upper management of the postal service. What's really transpiring is that management at a high level in the bureaucracy is causing most of the problems at local facilities. They are trying to force the public to make fewer appearances at the local stations, hoping that people will use stamp vending machines, the USPS website, and other venues.

The continued reduction of staff who come in direct contact with the public helps increase management incentive pay by showing a savings in costs, even if service goes to pot.

Because of this insulting treatment, which may be going on all across America, plenty of people are looking for alternatives.

With the changing times, in common usage are fax machines, UPS and other competitive delivery services, more attractive telephone services, email, and the Internet. Three reasons for the successes of alternative services are generally lower prices, America's incredible ingenuity and technology, and more customer-friendly environments.

However, there is another trend developing in America which is going to deal a lot of misery to millions of people in the future, a trend so current that most people haven't even thought about it, or don't want to think about it. It is the trend toward greater and greater security.

America is in a war. Regardless of what happens in Iraq, we will be dealing with a war on terrorism for many years. In an attempt to stop terrorism as it relates to travel in America, we are likely to have more problems than we realize.

People in many cities have always considered their airport as simply that, *their* airport. And in most cases, the people living in the surrounding communities and the entire region consider it *their* airport.

Right now we have plenty of security at airport facilities, but that security is federal. A facility is local, but for the smooth flow of operations, a wider view is necessary. And any time we give a federal agency a way to expand, we are asking for trouble.

How many bottlenecks can be created by low-level, federal bureaucrats simply wanting to show their authority by slowing down the process? Or how many people does it take to look over the shoulders of the few people actually working to satisfy the federal security guidelines, whatever they might be?

If longer security lines develop as a result of a few workers working while increasingly excessive supervision slows down the orderly process, what will be done to expedite the moving of the traveling public to aircraft doors?

In all likelihood the answer will be to increase already bloated security staffs to even more bloated and even less efficient operations. My prediction for the future is that we will see at many airports a security bureaucracy that will cause more Americans to stay home or take the car.

It is inevitable that at least some of our airports will face intentional slowdowns. Don't be surprised when many travelers who would normally consider flying to cities perhaps 300 to 500 miles away will choose to drive rather than be hassled by a small group of low-level bureaucrats who might not be having a good day and simply want to prove they have authority.

Think of the effect of allowing a federal bureaucracy to dictate the timeframe for all air travelers across America. It makes standing in line at that postal "service" line, delayed by one bureaucrat, look like a bag of nuts in a peanut butter factory.

Since 9/11, air passengers have become captive customers subjected to scanning by metal detectors, having their carry-on luggage x-rayed every time they board an airplane, and sometimes embarrassing and time-consuming searches. So far, this scrutiny has been fairly well accepted by the public as a necessary nuisance.

But airport security programs are not administered by the airports, and as we have learned, agencies can become bureaucracies. What will happen if these agencies decide to grow, to build empires, to perpetuate their existence through the usual methods? Imagine more security agents, perhaps additional check stations, and low-level bureaucrats deciding to impede the whole process so they can hire more low-level bureaucrats who will further impede the flow of passengers. This series of unfortunate events is coming soon to an airport near you.

Just this week a couple of events reinforced the bureaucracy problem in my mind. I took a flight from Houston to Amarillo, arriving at the terminal when almost nobody was showing up for flights. I was the only person in line when I handed my boarding pass and driver's license to the federal security employee. He took it and held it while he carried on a conversation with another security employee. They talked about personal stuff for perhaps a minute and a half. He finally looked at what I handed him and shoved it back toward me. He never acknowledged I was there by saying one word. I had interrupted his day and his actions made that very clear.

Here's another example to prove that the airline security bureaucracy has already started being created. Count the number of federal employees on hand that appear to be serving no purpose, except to tell you what you did wrong. How many times have you seen signs to take off your shoes and put them into the basket to go through the scanner? How many times have you seen a sign telling you to get all items out of your pockets and put them into the basket? How about a sign that says to have your driver's license ready, or that these small containers of liquids must be removed from those clear plastic bags they are required to be in and placed with your shoes and personal items to be scanned?

The answer to all these questions is simple. They don't put signs up to tell you what you will need to do so they can place more people there to tell you what you did wrong. This is called overstaffing, or pyramid building, resulting in an ever-growing massive bureaucracy. And these situations at airports across America can only increase.

Airports are continuing to attempt to overcome the logjams, as the air carriers try to expedite matters with creative programs such as curbside baggage checks, e-tickets, convenient parking, and centralized concourses. However, airports that were designed to handle a large number of passengers in an efficient manner can be sabotaged by intentionally created bureaucratic nonsense.

If the airlines, some of which are already experiencing financial trouble due to the cost of jet fuel, lose more money and have to be bailed out of trouble by the federal government, then the taxpayers will be called on to save an industry that was destroyed by federal bureaucracy. How ironic!

One last little story. Back to Yankton. I checked into a motel and the red message light on my phone was flashing. I listened to a message where a lady was calling another lady. She said it was very important that the second lady contact her "Because there is something I need you to *start*. Call me immediately when you get back."

Then there was a second message from the same lady. I don't usually listen to other people's phone calls, but I didn't know who they were, they would never know I listened, it was highly intriguing, and it was far better than afternoon TV. "What you need to do is think of a project to start up there. Start something that you can spend money on. Come up with an idea, get a group together, get a lunch together, get everybody there and then tell them about the program that you want *to start*. Whatever it is, make sure you spend

$5,000."

I have no idea which agency they were working for, or hoping to grab money from, but they desperately wanted to create a "need" that would spend $5,000, probably because they were close to the end of their budget year and wanted to make certain that all the money would be spent. And no telling what scheme they proposed and started, or how much the entire budget is costing taxpayers each year.

And if this innocent looking corruption is going on in Yankton, South Dakota, it's everywhere.

If there's any one thing the American people have become considerably more aware of in recent years, it's the expansion of the federal bureaucracy. There has been plenty of expansion of power, whether it's legal or not, by numerous agencies. In many cases that radical increase in control by various agencies took place even without additional congressional legislation.

America, at least in the view of many so-called national leaders, must always look to the federal government for both knowledge and guidance. Take for example the Environmental Protection Agency (EPA). The belief of that out-of-control agency is that Americans couldn't possibly have the knowledge or even the common sense required to safeguard our nation's natural resources. To them, not only are the American people totally inept, our elected national leaders have no knowledge in matters of the environment.

The reason I have zeroed in on the EPA is because it is the most flagrant of all the federal bureaucratic agencies at openly defying a cross section of the general population in this country.

The EPA couldn't care less about utilizing common sense. They have no respect for private property rights or the sovereignty of any state or its resources. And above all else, the EPA has total disdain for business of almost any sort. The one thing the EPA does have, though, is an affair going with the environmental movement.

We have people throughout this nation that take pride in protecting the natural resources of America. We care about our water, which I consider to be of the utmost value, our air, our wildlife, our croplands, our recreational lands, and our communities. We want very much to have lands that support wildlife and produce food. Even with all these things Americans work to preserve, the EPA is still of the opinion that the average American is so ignorant that we must look to their agenda, whatever it may be, for all the answers.

Why does this agency almost declare war on private property owners? Through the years, we have witnessed the totally insane decisions made to "protect" our environment. The most well known event was the protection of the spotted owl, not to mention the Rough Fish that caused thousands of farms to cease being productive in the Western states. Then there was a snail that demanded supreme protection. And we can't forget the Lesser Prairie-Chicken, evidently now threatened in several states. Has it ever occurred to our bureaucrats that there is one other threatened species: the owners of private lands in America? In the final analysis, we have found that the EPA simply doesn't care if land is privately owned.

For whatever it might be worth, we have heard a lot of discussion in America about eliminating programs created by the federal government, programs that might have been created to address a "temporary" problem. There is no such thing as a temporary federal program in America. They are all perpetual and growing in scope and budget each year. At least the states exercise some judgment in actually considering the elimination of programs. Not at the national level though.

When considering the elimination of federal programs that are leading this nation into total bankruptcy, let's keep one factor in mind. Individuals and groups, depending upon their political philosophy, want programs eliminated which benefit some other group — and vice versa. I openly admit that in most cases there is both justification to continue any federal agency in existence and justification to end that same agency. However, in the case of the EPA there need not be any debate. The EPA must be totally eliminated. Let's start over by simply addressing real and important environmental issues.

I remind you that private property in America throughout our history, until very recent years, has always been perceived as private property. How has this nation evolved into the situations we now face as owners? It's obvious that we haven't yet gone through a period in which an out-of-control government sends troops into our homes and lands, where the soldiers throw us out and take possession. But we do have out-of-control regulatory agencies telling us how we can't use land we own.

Just think about this scenario. You and your family own a piece of land that might very well have been in the family for generations. The one common belief, during all those years of family/ancestral ownership, is that the property is "owned." There was never a period of time, until very recent years, that any member of the family didn't believe that since the land was owned, they could do with it whatever they pleased.

Where are we today? Even without actual legislation enacted by Congress, regulatory agencies simply think they have the right to control your land. So answer this question for me: If the land is owned by you but someone else tells you what you can or cannot do with it, just what is your ownership worth?

Entire communities and even industries have been destroyed by regulatory agencies that found something in a law that, according to them, gave them control of properties and destinies. In many cases that perceived authority was simply created by them because of some vague language in the law.

I want to give you a good example of just how bad things have become in only the past few years, but first I want to make sure that you understand my position in this matter. I am in the oil and gas business and obviously am interested in the subject of energy in America. I also live in an area in which there is massive growth in wind energy projects. However, I own no interest in wind energy projects. More importantly though is the fact that oil, gas and wind energy compete with the coal industry. For the record, I have no business interests in coal, nor does any of my family. In addition to that, I have no family at all living in a coal-producing area of America. With my position stated, let's discuss the coal industry and regulators.

There are plenty of states in this country with communities that were largely supported economically because of coal mining. In many cases small communities throughout modern history were almost totally dependent on coal for their income. It was the reason people lived there, why local stores existed, how taxes were created and, above all else, why jobs existed. How is it then, that after decades of families spending their lives in a single industry, that all of a sudden they are considered to be anti-American, and guilty of trying to destroy the nation? The reason is quite simple. We now have out-of-control regulatory agencies, backed by the full force of our own tax dollars, that are carrying out whatever schemes, founded on reality or not, that they are determined to win. Always keep in mind that no matter how they win, in the final analysis they are expanding their power.

Let's now go to an industry related to coal, the coal-fired electric power plants. In the recent years numerous coal-fired power plants have been forced to cease operations. Many of those plants had been in operation for decades. Whenever a plant has to shut down, there's no need for the supply of coal that had previously been purchased. The end result is no power, no mining and no jobs. The reason for the shutdowns? In almost every case it would have cost a fortune to bring the facility into compliance with new rules instituted by the regulatory agency.

The agency's belief was that the plant was guilty of pollution. I want everybody to know what my opinion is concerning this subject. The so-called pollution in America is nothing when compared to the pollution around the world. Why are we addressing a perceived global problem by destroying our plants, communities and people while nothing is being done to honestly address this problem on a worldwide basis?

Here's the major reason for America taking this disastrous course. We have plenty of politicians that like to see regulators operate in out-of-control ways in order that the federal government can dictate policies to Americans.

There is one more subject to discuss relating to the bureaucracy. This subject is so new that the "quiet discussion" only started taking place in the past few months. The nature of this subject is really scary.

There have been a few comments made by politicians on the subject of which level of government should determine the outcome of any dispute. Here is what's evolving now: There's a theory that any matter in dispute must be settled on the basis where federal authority always supersedes state authority. This belief is that whatever any state says, and whatever law a state creates, means nothing if it conflicts with federal law or federal interpretation.

My question to you: If this theory is enacted and becomes the standard in America, why do we need states at all? Has America come to the point that individual states have no sovereignty whatsoever?

Chapter 5

An Overview of the U.S. and Us

In this chapter, we will cover a lot of territory. Most of the topics will be enlarged by my opinions, based on what I have observed. However, please keep in mind that I ran for federal office so I had to do extensive study on these issues. In each case that I discuss, you may be able to think of similar situations.

Throughout modern history, America has been referred to by various names and descriptions. To the rest of the world we have tried to describe what our system is: a democracy, "the land of the free," a free enterprise system, or "the land of opportunity" where a person can enjoy "the American Dream," which requires further definition since it means different things to different people. But the dream to create opportunity, to recreate ourselves within an environment free from persecution, is what brought our forefathers to this nation from every other nation in the world. Our greatness is not only in what we accomplish, it is also in the variety of expressions that we allow to go on, as long as an individual's expression does not greatly limit someone else's expression. From our desire to be free has evolved the free enterprise system, successful for so many years.

Millions of Americans face some tough times in their lives as they try to make their dream come true. Over the centuries, millions tried but no matter how hard they worked, it simply never happened, sometimes due to forces outside their control: war, depression, discrimination, indifference, or cruelty. Americans are, as a rule, idealistic but imperfect people.

We as a nation have survived wars, depressions, economic downturns, floods, tornados, hurricanes, fires, droughts, infestations, earthquakes, blizzards, and other disasters. The wars were really bad, but we survived them. We *used to be* a nation with plenty of determination to overcome whatever happens. That was the national will.

America today has limited pride in itself. Again, by no stretch of the imagination, do I imply that all of us fit into any mold. But unfortunately, a sizeable percentage of our people have absolutely no pride in this nation whatsoever.

If there is a reason why pride has become so unimportant to so many, I would have to say that it certainly goes right back to the main subject of this book, the Buffet Syndrome, and a general lack of responsibility toward our neighbors. Easy Street has perhaps become too easy, and we have grown lazy, or at least indifferent about where we get our money.

On the bright side, isn't it heartwarming to see someone take pride in their family, one of their children, the way they do their job, or the company they work for? Or hear stories about how someone helped another person less fortunate, especially when the helper could use some help.

I recall one time when my wife and I were at lunch, in of all places, a pizza buffet. A teenager, who appeared to be the son of one of the owners, was cleaning up the tables. He was working hard, doing an excellent job, and wearing a big smile. It was so refreshing to see a young man doing the very best that he possibly could, and he made me feel good.

Although it was a buffet without waiters or waitresses, and customers were expected to refill their own drinks, I left him a tip simply because it was so nice to see him doing his best and being so happy about it. I would do the same thing again if I ran into him today.

Let's talk about rights and responsibilities. America has a

huge problem because we have millions of people who think they have plenty of rights and no responsibilities whatsoever. However, they are simply throwing their lives away. There is no question that not everyone has money, a good formal education, equal opportunity, or even good health. But it is my opinion that most Americans want to see people succeed in their lives. We want the opportunities in this country to be utilized by those who have the desire to accomplish something which will give them pride, hope, and self-esteem for themselves and their families.

I would like to tell you a story about someone who had the odds against her, but because she accepted responsibility and wanted to provide for her family, she accomplished what she set out to do.

I was in television news at the time. I moderated a weekday news/interview program at noon. The local community college, Amarillo College, had a curriculum for people of all ages. One was the "Access Program," established to help adults get started in a formal education program.

The head of the Access Program appeared on my show, along with an unmarried lady who had just entered the program as a student. With three small children to support, no high school diploma, and a part-time job that paid very little, she was currently receiving temporary financial assistance in her education program so that her family would have a place to live and food to eat. She was very happy to be able to get an education.

Here is the best part. Some five years later I got a phone call. A lady told me her name and recounted her appearance on my show. I remembered her. She just wanted me to know what had happened in her life since then.

She had gotten her associate degree from Amarillo College and a bachelor's degree from a nearby university. She now had a good job and was enrolling at the university to earn her master's degree.

The odds were against that lady, yet she managed to

achieve everything she wanted by accepting responsibility for her life and utilizing opportunities. What I find amazing, though, is that millions of people simply make no genuine attempt to improve their lives. They do not take advantage of educational opportunities. Or they refuse to utilize their talents in a trade or profession — they aren't even motivated to begin a project, much less complete one. I find it amazing that some people in America simply accept having nothing as being their destiny. How is it that any human being can be content knowing that as he looks around his neighborhood, city, and county, his position in life is miserable and will likely remain so if he doesn't do something?

Have we as a nation so brainwashed a significant section of our people into believing they have no value at all? Perhaps a better question might be, just what have we done as a nation to encourage people to actively participate in America? It strikes me that we have done an excellent job of sending precisely the wrong message.

I have seen many instances where a person throws away a productive life to settle into a welfare existence. I would much prefer to see a person utilize even one available opportunity or start developing a tiny talent.

Millions of people in America make no effort to manage the one thing they have plenty of: time. This is one subject that I can speak on with some authority because I believe it is a life lesson I have learned. And I sincerely hope that you or some member of your family will benefit from the examples I am going to relate to you.

When I was 37 years old, I was a full-time news director on the day shift of a television station. I really wanted to accomplish something in my life; I enjoyed working at the station, but all of us seem to have built into us a longing to strive for something higher. Although a high school graduate, I had only taken a few college courses while in the service. My evenings were available for something besides watching television. There was one small room isolated from most of the other rooms, where I would often find myself listening to a radio station that played easy-listening music.

What I realized was that I had an opportunity before me. It made a lot more sense to get an education than to waste my time each evening during the week. That small, quiet room, and soft music to study by, would be perfect. So I registered at Amarillo College.

Two years later I graduated with an Associate's Degree in Mid-Management by attending night classes. All I really did was manage my time. Think about all the people who could do the same thing. Think about all the people who live in cities with a community college near them and have the time to attend.

What if we could turn around the lives of, say, a million Americans — maybe 10 million? How would America be affected if 10 million people turned from being time wasters into life winners, people who accomplish what they were born to do? They would turn from the ranks of the unemployed to employed workers in environments they are proud of and enjoy, own homes, drive nice automobiles. Commitment creates pride and self-esteem. All this can be accomplished by managing time.

My college experience worked so well that some 10 years later I again made the decision to better manage my time — probably the most important decision of my life. Unlike the fellow who was given the opportunity of a lifetime to start a construction business but failed because he wouldn't manage his time, I wanted my life to be a success story.

In 1986 the bottom fell out of the oil and gas business. Most oil and gas companies in the Texas Panhandle went out of business.

I had been dabbling in the investments business. Rather than turn away from oil and gas, I saw an opportunity to take advantage of the significant downturn and buy even more because everything was relatively cheap. But, what to buy? The key would lie in hours and hours of *research* to identify the best potential targets. I knew I could find them, *providing* I did the research. In other words, I had to manage my time outside my normal working hours.

I made a decision. I loved watching professional football. Sunday was my day for football, from the time the first game was on TV in the afternoon until the last game ended that night. And Monday night football was also always on my agenda.

I decided to quit watching football completely and spend those same hours researching, and subsequently acquiring, interests in oil and gas properties. I knew that if I was successful in accomplishing my goal, it would be much more productive than watching football.

All I can say is this: I haven't watched football in 18 years and the rewards for utilizing my time are beyond measure. I am now financially, and emotionally, comfortable for the rest of my life. When I talk about the value of people managing their time, it's not an empty theory I came up with; it's what I have done in my life. And there are plenty of people in America whose lives can improve dramatically simply by dedicating time to some meaningful goal.

It's also important to point out that the time was only one day and one evening each week. As it turns out, there were almost no interruptions since I wasn't subject to the usual constant diversions of the normal office routine. I estimate that the hours spent in research were easily four times as productive as I hoped they would be. Just think of how productive some of your free time could be.

The lady who went to college despite all hardships took responsibility for her life, and so did I. We did not assume we had unlimited rights but no responsibilities. Two words that go together as surely as "love and marriage" are "rights and responsibilities."

Two words that have different meanings yet are often interchanged nowadays are "rights" and "entitlements." Every citizen of the United States of America has certain *rights*, established in the Constitution and the Bill of Rights. They are well-known and form the very basis of our philosophy as a nation. Some people even claim one or more of these rights when they are not eligible, like terrorists who plot to destroy our country but hide behind the Constitution when caught.

However, for a person to be *entitled* to a specific program established by Congress, funded, and administered, a person must meet the requirements. If eligible for benefits, we say that person is "entitled."

All Americans have the freedom of speech. They can criticize the government and the President all they want to and not fear reprisal. That is their right. If a person cannot read, and a government program exists to teach reading, that person is entitled to take the course.

Just as some temporary taxes have a way of becoming permanent, some programs exist so long that people forget that they were created to solve a specific problem, and they expect the programs always to be there. For example, the welfare program to help provide housing for people who need affordable rent, has been around so long that many people believe cheap or free housing is their right.

Many people believe they have a right to a driver's license. They are *entitled* to a license, after passing the proper tests established by the law.

Millions of families are caught up in the welfare trap. When I refer to the term "welfare trap," that is exactly what I mean. It traps people to the point that there is no motivation to ever improve their lifestyle.

People caught in the welfare trap probably didn't get into the trap by being involved in just one entitlement program. The fewer programs a welfare family is involved in, the more likely they can get out.

The trap is set when people find an additional program, or programs, available for them through the notification requirement. Agencies inform people about other agencies' programs for which they can attempt to qualify.

At some point in time, after signing up for everything possible, many people believe there is no other option to welfare. It is not likely that a poor family, utilizing all the programs possible, is going to look for any other alternative.

Even if a mother with three small children, for example, is able to work and wants to get a job, circumstances prevent it. With all the benefits being received at no cost and without any tax consequences, she can't take a job unless it is considerably greater than her welfare check and carries significant employee benefits. She might really have the desire to accomplish something for herself and her three children, but she is hopelessly stuck in the trap.

Does anyone really think that continued or expanded programs for the poor will solve the problems of most families? The truth is that they only make matters worse.

Our hypothetical mother has a house to live in, utilities paid for, food on the table, and medical care provided, whether at a public clinic or the hospital emergency room. She will probably never try to improve herself as long as all that is available to her.

The irony is that after an extended period of time she will possibly begin to believe that she has the *absolute right* to all those benefits — not an entitlement, *a right*. And, having maintained that minimal existence for so long, she honestly thinks she never had a choice, never had a chance to improve her family's lives.

Situations like this are commonplace. They are also becoming an acceptable way to live. What about the kids who witness their parents stuck in the welfare trap? What are the chances the kids will ever accept personal responsibility leading toward self-respect, ever have any discipline or any desire to succeed?

This also applies to what I will simply refer to as entities: states, cities, or counties that want a bigger piece of the "federal pie" — what are affectionately called "pork barrel" programs.

One of the items I mentioned in 2007 was food stamps. That subject, along with a multitude of other federal programs, is still worthy of discussion seven years later. Since the nature of my current edition is to relate to America the growth in federal government and federal programs during this short period of time, I think you will be surprised to look at the statistical data. You would think that America is in an economic depression.

The food stamp program started as a pretty simple deal. People managed to qualify for assistance in purchasing food simply by receiving the standardized food stamp coupons. Those coupons were used just like cash at grocery stores, rather than handing dollar bills to the checkout employee. Those food stamps could only purchase basic food items.

Where are we today in the program? We now refer to the program as the Supplemental Nutrition Assistance Program, or SNAP. Using the coupon program supposedly no longer embarrasses people. Quite the contrary. In the event you happen to be standing in line waiting for someone to use the Lone Star card here in Texas, in all probability you won't know that you have just been witnessing purchases made with what used to be food stamps. And there's a possibility that you also witnessed more than the purchase of basic food items.

It seems strange to me that items such as soft drinks, candy, cookies, cakes and ice cream are considered as qualifying items in a program called Supplemental Nutrition Assistance. I do recall recently witnessing a lady who attempted to purchase dog food with the Lone Star card. The clerk said that the dog food didn't qualify. That lady then handed a very high-priced steak to the clerk and said, "Then I'll feed this to my dog." That item did qualify.

Here are the most recent costs to operate SNAP. These figures come from page 94 of the 2014 *World Almanac and Book of Facts*. In 2008, that cost was $37,640,000,000. In 2012 the cost was $78,437,000,000. That's a 108 percent increase in the cost of the program in only four years. This is almost unbelievable, but it's reality.

My question to you is this: Has the economy in America gotten so bad in only a four-year period (2008-2012) that the number of people qualifying for what used to be the Food Stamp Program should have more than doubled? Personally, I think not.

Other than the fact that America is facing a disaster economically, because of pure debt and political posturing, there's another trend taking place that will insure the failure of any nation. I feel obligated to explain to you that of all the subjects discussed in this book, that this trend is a planned event, and as such, is one of the most important.

This nation, through its leaders, political philosophers, and above all else, millions of citizens, are combining to destroy America. No, it isn't just inept leadership. In reality, it's the millions of people, with the help of an out-of-control government, that's insuring the failure of America.

Here's what's really taking place — and the truth hurts because it's really an indictment of millions of Americans. The trend is this: People are in fact, planning their lives around entitlement programs. It's certainly not an isolated situation, occurring only in certain geographic areas or income groups or ethnic groups. People from all walks of life, including entire families, actually seek a year-to-year lifestyle based upon federal programs. They are of the opinion that they can live a better life, on an ongoing basis, simply by seeking and qualifying for multiple programs, all of which are paid for by others.

Their attitude is, "Why would an individual, or family, want to work at a low-paying job, have to meet a work schedule, pay household rent and bills, buy food, and pay for medical care?" From their point of view, working doesn't make sense. America has now evolved into a society in which we reward people for choosing to do nothing.

We qualify most anyone for the food stamp program, W.I.C. cards, subsidized rent, subsidized utilities, completely free medical care and other miscellaneous direct assistance programs. In addition to that, there are many local assistance programs. It's gotten to the point that a family planning a welfare career is eager to place their children in public schools, which have become little more than taxpayer-paid-for day care centers, including all meals. All of this is being actively engaged in by millions of Americans and millions of American families.

At the same time, another activity is taking place in Washington and at the various bureaucracies to service all the direct benefit programs underway. We are now witnessing how politicians and bureaucrats measure success. They consider programs that grow in size, cost, and participation as being successful. Their belief is that more people are being served.

Here in October 2014, we are witnessing a low unemployment rate in America. Politicians are bragging about it. The truth is, this a phony number. Millions of people choose to totally live on multiple welfare programs, wouldn't take a job if it was offered to them, don't want to be bothered by looking for a job, and get much more in entitlement income than what a job would provide.

Even more Americans are intentionally engaging in the Buffet Syndrome by educating themselves. People with good educations and good incomes are researching ways to qualify for government programs at no cost, programs that they might have previously been paying to participate in. In short, they are learning to "work the system."

And while this is underway by an increasingly larger percent of the population, the government is helping them by sending out mailings and establishing physical facilities to instruct people in one area: How they might, or could, qualify at absolutely no cost for a program that they have been paying to participate in.

With this in mind, do you think there's even the slightest opportunity that things will change?

The federal budget, which is nothing short of a national disgrace, isn't doing any favors for the people in this country or for most of the entities within our nation. Not only is the notification requirement included in each federally created program destroying individuals, in many cases it simply points out the lack of business judgment, or the hypocrisy, of many elected officials at the various levels.

As the federal government encourages families to settle for a minimal standard of living and not take some responsibility for their lives, it possesses so much power through the nation's purse strings that it can impose extremely expensive financial mandates on local entities, occasionally throwing them a few crumbs by rewarding them with some questionable little pork barrel program.

Our hypothetical mother and others in her area are able to receive so much through local entities, who are happy to take a few crumbs from the federal table, even if they have to use local funds to oversee the administration of federally mandated programs or guidelines, and knowing the need for local tax dollars will always increase as the bloated federal budget puts the squeeze on local entities to fund truly necessary programs.

Would a local entity lose respect for itself by taking a few federal dollars to fund a pork barrel project, a very questionable need, simply because the cost might only be 10 percent local funds and 90 percent federal funds? I don't think so. Probably every entity considers itself necessary and can point to others it considers unnecessary.

When will many of our independent school districts throughout the United States tell the federal bureaucracy to use federal funds to administer mandated programs or guidelines?

At what point do the school districts insist that states have rights, districts have rights, and teachers are educators, not bureaucrats? Bureaucracy in a local school system is a huge hindrance to education.

I do know that many of our teachers are concerned about what is happening in our schools. Without a doubt, some teachers would prefer to be in administration, but plenty of teachers prefer to spend their time in the classroom.

When will many of our so-called independent school districts throughout the United States tell the federal bureaucracy to use federal funds to administer mandated programs or guidelines?

There is one story about education that I will never forget. Years ago while running for Congress, I had the occasion to meet a man who was greatly concerned about what kids were, and were not, being taught in school. I would rather not mention his name, only say that he was a veterinarian in Dalhart, a city of about 7,000 in the Panhandle of Texas. He had been on the Dalhart Independent School District's Board for several years.

He remarked that during the 12 years of attendance there was something the children were never taught. When I asked what that was, he said, "The free enterprise system." In other words, what America is.

In 12 years there was no course or even part of a course devoted to that topic. He was so concerned about that void in their education that he did something about it.

He showed me a small paperback book, green in color. He said that a few weeks prior to school letting out for the summer, he would get a list of all the graduating seniors and would call their parents, making an appointment to meet with them and their child one evening.

While in the homes of those graduates he would tell the

seniors and their parents, "This is what was never taught to you in school, what made America great. Capitalism and the free enterprise system made America the land of opportunity, created a strong economy, and a freedom for people." He purchased those books out of his own pocket.

Since most graduating seniors are about 18 years old yet have had little or no education in America's free enterprise system during their 12 years of schooling, how are they to acquire some knowledge of what fuels the nation's economy? It's my belief that parents play a key role. After all, the majority of families have been engaged in making a living while the kids grew up, so parents are a huge influence on them, which can be either very good or really bad.

I would like to take this opportunity to tell you a story regarding America's free enterprise system, the influence of parents in their children's lives, and the great things that can be accomplished by kids.

My family is well aware that I have made my own living since a young child. I would be the first to admit that it was much easier years ago for a youngster to get a job than it is today, especially considering potential employers' concerns about contingent liabilities associated with hiring young kids and ambulance-chasing lawyers always on the prowl.

When my youngest son was around 10, he asked me a simple question. It went something like this: "Dad, when you were a kid my age, you had a job. Why can't I get a job and make some money myself?" I first told him it was about impossible in more recent history for someone to hire somebody his age because of potential liabilities. He dismissed that, asking again what he could do to make some money.

As it turns out, the timing couldn't have been better. I had an idea for him and it has had an effect on him all his life. Only two or three days prior to our conversation, I was carrying the trash out to the alley and about to throw it into the dumpster. I looked down into the dumpster and saw a large stack of advertising papers — at least 200 of them, possibly as many as 500. Yes, they were full-color brochures, flyers to be placed in the doors of area homes. Someone had obviously been paid to distribute them, yet had chosen to donate them to the dump.

I told my son that he could start his own business. Slover's Flyer Service was born: a door-to-door flyer delivery service. After having business cards printed, he went to neighborhood businesses and asked them what messages they would like to get out to neighbors in the immediate trade area. He would then go to a printer and have the flyers printed. The last step was simply to distribute those flyers in the areas designated by his customers.

In his sales pitch to possible clients, I told my son to say this: Each and every one of the flyers will be placed at someone's door. There will not be any left over or disposed of, and only one placed in each door.

That is precisely how my son ran his creative and highly ethical business. To this day, over 20 years later, he has always been totally honest, creative, and ethical in everything he does, just like he was in running that little business as a kid. I have always told my children and my business associates to be ethical in everything they do, including how they run a business. My kids are well aware that there are plenty of opportunities to engage in America's free enterprise system by being honest, creative, and ethical.

One of the things millions of Americans take for granted is education. We all have an opportunity to get a high school education. While it seems that many people place no value on becoming educated, there are still many countries in the world where educational opportunities are virtually nonexistent.

During the war in Vietnam, many refugees fled to the United States. I recall a period of time during which many of those refugee families were making a place for themselves within communities throughout the United States. There are two situations I would like to relate to you.

You probably have seen where a basically non-English

speaking family operates a business, perhaps a small restaurant. Think about the long hours they work, and perhaps the small rooms in which the entire family lives. What really impresses me the most is this: For several years I read with interest in the Amarillo newspaper about the Vietnamese children graduating from the high schools at the top of the class. It was heartwarming, to say the least, when these first-generation Americans with Vietnamese, Cambodian, and Laotian surnames had applied themselves, not only graduating with honors, but learning American culture and a new language at the same time!

In contrast, is it possible that most Americans take things for granted to the point that they can't really recognize the value of learning? Fortunately, the number of people who appear to have given up, have no pride, take no responsibility, and possibly have no self-respect are only a minority.

I got to know a Japanese family living in Amarillo, observing their progress for at least 15 years. When I first met the father, mother, and two daughters, they had a small restaurant. One of the daughters spoke English well enough to be understood most of the time. The younger daughter spoke some English but was extremely difficult to communicate with. The mother and father spoke only Japanese.

Amarillo at that time had a technical training institute. I was asked by the oldest daughter to assist a Japanese student at that facility. The problem was this: That student, along with about eight others, was near the end of their allowable stay in the United States before having to return to Japan. They were having to learn English in addition to their technical training; there were hardly enough hours in the day for them to assimilate all this information. They had no life at all, only themselves.

I managed to get their stay in the United States extended so they could graduate from the program. They stuck it out. They all lived together, had little or no contact with the world, no social life; they wanted one thing and one thing only: an education.

Our greatness is not arrived at by government regulators, a huge bureaucracy, or even monstrous outlays for questionable programs to "help" people succeed in their private lives or workplaces, nor from the federal government constantly teasing people in local communities with a few measly tax dollars returning to them in the form of direct aid programs. It is our determination to succeed despite all obstacles in a capitalist system that allows for achievement, if effort is applied.

I would like to tell you a story about a typical pork barrel project for a local entity. My office is in a strip mall. Immediately across the street is a walking trail, a concrete path built over what at one time were railway tracks owned by what is commonly known as The Rock Island — actually the full name is The Chicago, Rock Island and Pacific Railroad.

The trail runs several miles, but only on very rare occasions have I seen anyone walking there. In fact, if a person drives to the path, there is no place to park their vehicle. It is not even worth much as a sidewalk.

The walking trail was constructed with 10 percent local funds and 90 percent state funds: a classic pork barrel project that I am reminded of every day.

Had a local entity voted to pay for this boondoggle with local tax dollars, what response do you think it would have gotten from taxpayers? I can see in my mind a probable editorial in the local newspaper, closing on this line: "This project is not a necessary expenditure of *anybody's* tax dollars!"

The entire system of creation, administration, and notification of federal programs is so fatally flawed that one could say the *concept itself* is one big pork barrel program. If the truth about federal funding of entitlement programs ever becomes totally understood by the majority of the American people, they will demand a restructuring of the system. The current system *guarantees* waste, each year bestowing more benefits on more people, entrapping a greater number of families into the welfare pit. The system cannot help eliminate welfare in the United States because there is no reason for any recipient who is able to maintain a minimal lifestyle with no responsibilities to attempt anything else.

Here is the story of two very different nations. Think of all the people living in border towns in Mexico. Many of the families, in spite of all that they do to survive, might be lucky to have anything to live in or anything to eat. Whereas, an average American welfare family probably has a standard of living higher than most of the border town families.

Both deal in harsh realities, but the difference is that one family's plight continues in spite of the fact that they do everything in their power to change it, while the other does nothing.

You may think that I am just disgusted with poor people. That's not true. I am disgusted with a system that is broken and has ultimately failed. I have no respect for a politically motivated bureaucratic system that destroys pride in people by taking away their initiative and is so big, so out of touch with reality, that many people who badly need assistance simply can't get it.

We have in America many truly needy people of all ages, who, no matter how hard they try, simply cannot sustain themselves — such as the physically or mentally handicapped. We have people who have worked hard all their lives but because of a serious health issue are locked out of the system. I am sincere in stating that there are plenty of people in America who absolutely need help and should receive it.

With that in mind, let's move to a subject that may ruffle a few feathers on a lot of people, including a few "experts." We need to ask, at what point does the irresponsibility of people become the responsibility of society? At what point does political correctness border on the irrational? Have we transitioned into a nation in which people are never at fault, no matter what they do? Let's discuss a few common areas of concern.

Do you recall years ago when "drunks" would be picked up and placed in jail a few nights because they had been obnoxious to people in public areas? As a general rule, they were allowed to dry out at taxpayers' expense for a short while. Many times, upon being released they were encouraged to find another area in which to hang out.

While we still have drunk drivers arrested across the nation each day, we seldom have "drunks" arrested. What we have today are labeled alcoholics. I guess they all got promoted and now they are medical patients, some of whom live on the streets rather than in medical facilities.

Isn't it amazing that America has apparently made progress in dealing with some problems? In this case an extraordinary transition has taken place: We have identified many people diagnosed with the disease of alcoholism while at the same time eradicated all the drunks.

We have also faced the reality that all those drunks we eliminated were not at fault for what they had become; since they were really alcoholics, they had no control over drinking.

Are we so foolish, and so politically correct in this country, to believe that the only reason a drunk ever started drinking to begin with was because he was afflicted with a disease called alcoholism when he was but a child? And why is society to blame for his problems?

Many years ago I was a chain smoker. Although I quit smoking 42 years ago, I can still relate to anyone with a habit that is tough to deal with, and tougher to break. And at the time, I had a job where I had to work three different shifts each week — two day shifts followed by two evening shifts, then a midnight. My schedule was erratic, at best.

For years I smoked three full packs of cigarettes every day, except for the Thursday midnight shift. On Thursdays it was four packs. Smoking didn't help my pocketbook, either. The food in my family's kitchen cabinets was very basic, and not much of it. We barely survived.

I can recall going outside to my run-down car in the middle of the night to dig cigarette butts out of the ashtray. I would straighten them out and relight for a few puffs. I also recall cashing in soft drink and milk bottles to buy low-cost food. Somehow, I always had money for cigarettes.

When I quit smoking, I quit cold turkey. But for as long as five years after I quit, I would find myself reaching into my pocket for a cigarette that wasn't there. Why did I quit, when it was so difficult for me? That's simple: I knew it was incredibly stupid to smoke — hard on my budget and I was killing myself. But I never smoked another cigarette after the day I quit.

I still wonder about this. How can people who have almost nothing to begin with, continue smoking? We all know people who are barely subsisting yet continue to smoke. No longer are cigarettes cheap like they were 40 years ago, mostly because most states have imposed huge taxes in recent years.

I just stepped across the parking lot to check the price of cigarettes. On this day in Amarillo, Texas, they are $4.79 a pack. With sales tax, $5.19 *per pack*. Let's just say someone smokes two packs per day for a total of $10.00 a day, or $300 a month. If he makes $8.00 an hour and works 40 hours a week, or 4-1/3 weeks per month, he makes $1,385 per month before taxes and deductions. It makes absolutely no sense at all to continue a habit that absorbs a quarter of his after-tax income.

With money in mind, I have more questions. Why should taxpayers, his neighbors, be required to absorb all the medical costs of someone who, by choice, destroys his health? Why should hospital costs for a person who has smoked for many years be the responsibility of his community? Why should a public clinic be used to treat smoking-related conditions? Why should taxpayers pay disability to people who knew they were ruining their health? Why should taxpayers pay for long-term care in nursing homes for people with health problems solely caused by smoking?

Even 42 years ago I could see that if I continued smoking it would kill me — long before the true dangers of cigarette smoking were advertised. Yet I, and many millions of other quitters over the decades, figured it out. It would have been totally irresponsible for me not to quit.

The point to all this is that millions of people chose, and choose today, to be irresponsible, thinking that society will make certain that their minimal needs, including health care, will be met. They need to think further about their survivors, after they die early from cigarettes. What about the spouse who will be financially wrecked when he dies and she still has children at home? Why should children have to suffer, watching their moms and dads die, and perhaps not be able to attend college because there will not be any extra money in the family?

For a long time in this country the word "vices" referred to drinking and smoking; both have negative, and often fatal, impacts on people. But let's discuss an even worse abuse problem that America is dealing with: drugs.

There is no way I could even begin to cover all the ramifications of drugs in a book of this size, much less part of one chapter. The problem is so far-reaching that I would only scratch the surface if I wrote an entire book about it.

A couple of terms have changed in recent years. It has gotten to the point that we don't have many "dopers" any longer; we now have "victims of drug abuse." And yes, we now have "drug addicts," who, according to many politically correct spokespersons, are in fact, victims. I just find it strange that they are "victims" of a "disease," drug addiction, and supposedly are not responsible for what they do.

Yet in the eyes of society the people who get caught selling (trafficking) drugs probably should be held responsible for what they do. The consensus is that they are enablers, harming people who are victims or addicts.

At what point do addicts become traffickers in the drug world? It seems to me that a natural progression for a drug addict would be to become part of the drug supply chain, to sell drugs in order to get drugs for his own use. I wonder how many times a charge of trafficking has been reduced to possession in order to get a plea to the lesser charge and avoid going to trial.

If this scenario is correct, then how can we be so compassionate in dealing with someone charged with possession when in fact they might have just as easily been charged with the appropriate crime, drug trafficking, a crime America abhors and normally associates with a lengthy prison sentence?

In the meantime, crimes like burglaries are in large part being committed by drug abusers or drug addicts in order to have money to purchase drugs. I am still of the opinion that these people are, in plain and simple terms, dopers.

A series of questions come to mind when discussing these people, most of whom are quite young. Did they think they were immune to getting hooked on dope? Did they even consider the adverse impact upon their lives and families, which in many cases were mom and dad? Did they possibly think they were invincible? Did they consider exercising any responsibility for their actions? The final question is, did they even care?

Here's what has happened in the world of drug convictions, in no more than seven years. To begin with, a theory has been accepted that a person found with a very small quantity of marijuana doesn't really constitute being a criminal. Law enforcement now concentrates on prosecuting people found with huge stashes of marijuana, but more often than that, large quantities of hard drugs.

The second new thing to happen is that there's an opinion that someone brought to the police station for possession of drugs, whatever form of drugs they may be, hasn't committed a violent crime and as such, can be released from confinement. We have now witnessed many men and women, who could have easily been charged for drug trafficking ten years ago, are today only receiving a charge for possession and then turned loose. The reasons given: The person wasn't committing a violent crime, the prisons are already over-crowded, and the current view of society has softened concerning drugs, allowing him or her to stay free.

The third thing that has happened is that several states have legalized marijuana sales. We now have several states that welcome public sales of marijuana, not for medicinal purposes but recreational uses. Some states have also imposed big sales taxes on those sales.

Please allow me to sum up the topics in this chapter. Drinking, smoking, and drug use cost society and American taxpayers a bundle, including the huge costs to local governments and institutions. What is being accomplished? Nothing. The only thing we know for sure is that, as a nation, we are coddling bad behavior, and the more we coddle, the more widespread will be the problems.

Another reality of life in America is that the federal programs that were created to benefit many people have changed in purpose: Temporary assistance to help people through bad periods in their lives have become long-term subsidies, a way of life for millions that reduces self-respect and the hope for a better way. Local communities lose people who could be working and contributing economically. Those who are working pay higher taxes each year for ill-conceived programs.

Who benefits from the federal system? The truly needy who absolutely have no other options, such as the seriously handicapped, are in fact benefited, and they should be. The federal bureaucracy, which is constantly feeding at the public trough, engaging in the Buffet Syndrome, should not benefit. National politicians, who on a daily basis attempt to divide the people in order to perpetuate themselves in office, benefit the most. For many of them, had they not been able to control the funding and engage in political posturing, their political careers would have ended long ago.

I am thoroughly disgusted with politicians who sell out their country, diminish the value of people's lives, and even intentionally try to divide the nation along racial lines simply to perpetuate themselves in office. But in a later chapter I will discuss them in depth, and explain how you and I can at least attempt to deal with them.

I will end this chapter with one scary thought: As to the size of the federal government, and to a lesser extent, state government, there is no serious effort whatsoever being made to reduce the cost of government or the size of the bureaucracy, and there hasn't been in years.

Chapter 6

Legalized Extortion in America

There is no shortage of lawyers, or law firms, in the U.S. That is not just my opinion, though. It is an absolute fact, and so important that I have dedicated a whole chapter of this book to one single vocation. Why? Because the effects of having so many lawyers in America is far-reaching, and it is almost impossible to estimate how much it costs America to have this glut of lawyers, not to mention the lawyers who pervert the legal system.

Before I give my reasons for having a far less than favorable view of many in the legal profession, I think it is important to show the other side of the coin.

I deal with a lot of lawyers in my business and have for many years. I have a lawyer in my immediate family. The best friend I ever had was a lawyer. I employ lawyers several times a year. I am currently paying lawyers from two separate firms a considerable fee to deal with a very complex matter. I paid two other firms a considerable fee earlier this year.

There are plenty of good lawyers performing services for people that are absolutely necessary — quality professionals all across the U.S. On the other hand, there are some real scoundrels in the legal profession. A few years back, it was common to call them "ambulance chasers."

A few decades ago, a new lawyer announced his presence and new business by simply "hanging out the shingle" on his office door. Business would then grow and prosper as the lawyer's reputation and experience grew.

Things have changed dramatically, for the worse. The telephone directory *was once* simply a guide to locate a lawyer. A lawyer's name might have been in bold letters in either the white pages or yellow pages. In many states, advertising of legal services was not allowed by law.

Not so today. A few years ago, while going through the Las Vegas, Nevada, Yellow Pages, I was amazed to see so many ads for attorneys. It struck me that total space for lawyers far exceeded advertising space for casinos, hotels, entertainment venues, and other features in a city noted for being the entertainment capital in that part of the world.

And it's certainly not just Las Vegas that has plenty of advertising by lawyers. I have before me the Amarillo AT&T Directory, 2006 issue. I got curious enough to examine my hometown directory.

The total business section is 923 pages. The attorneys consume 48 pages in a city of some 180,000 people. That seems excessive to me, especially if we put it into context with other business advertising.

Plenty of buildings and automobiles exist in a city of 180,000. No telling how much money is involved in commerce relating to these two items alone. Think of the many thousands of transactions each week involving real property and automobiles.

So let's compare. The auto section, which includes everything relating to cars, is 29 pages. Real estate section is 12 pages. Homes, 19 pages. Buildings, 8 pages. Apartments, 3 pages. The total for all of these comes to 71. Compare that to 48 pages for attorneys only. This tells me that there are far more attorneys than the market should reasonably support.

With such a huge number of lawyers and law firms competing for business, there is no question that the legal system in the U.S. is in deep trouble. In addition, we are creating far more ambulance chasers. While thousands of lawyers go about their business each day, performing necessary legal services for their clients, many lawyers have become nothing more than ambulance chasers without an ambulance.

Some of the things a small minority of these lawyers do, and I really mean a very small minority, are so disgusting and so destructive that they don't deserve the respect of anyone.

Extensive advertising by attorneys has exceeded good taste. It is one thing to inform the public as to the area or areas of expertise of the firm, but another to advertise to the point of soliciting, or perhaps almost begging clients to file a lawsuit. Whenever advertising gets to the point that it encourages someone to file a suit for something simply because the person thinks there is a possibility of getting something for nothing, things have gone too far.

Let's talk about lawsuits and their effects on America. It has gotten to the point where many people make business decisions based simply upon contingent liabilities. Why should a person risk his future in any venture where lawsuits are being widely solicited?

Although I worked when I was very young, a businessman today would be taking a significant risk in hiring a juvenile in any business environment. So much for the kids' summer jobs that existed for decades in the past.

America used to be a world leader in manufacturing. Not any longer. Why would venture capitalists build a major factory in America today and take the chance of facing unlimited contingent liabilities?

I sometimes wonder why companies even *consider* locating a plant in America. Have you driven across the border into Mexico in the past few years? It's interesting to see how many American plants are located barely across the border.

There is absolutely no question that lower labor costs present a significant reason why companies locate facilities in foreign countries. And taxes can have a considerable impact on a manufacturing industry. These two factors, plus out-of-control corporate ambulance-chasing lawsuits, all but guarantee that we as a nation will continue driving businesses away from our land.

Believe it or not, lawsuits play a huge role in a manufacturing economy, or the lack of a manufacturing economy. Unfortunately, some television and newspaper ads show a lawyer describing various industries that people may have worked in or been around. It's a shopping list where someone might find some past association.

Then the ad presents the name of a medical condition and its symptoms. Perhaps only a few people have ever heard of that condition and most people can't even pronounce it, but some people will think, "What the heck? I might be able to get some cash for nothing." There's a toll-free number to call. "My lucky day! It won't cost one red cent to try for it!"

This is just how low some lawyers have sunk. They couldn't care less about the people being solicited. They will put huge fees in their pockets if the suit is successful, or settled, in addition to a percentage of the proceeds going to the "harmed" party.

Most of these ads are conducted on a national basis. National solicitation seems to get more respect than a lawyer with identical business ethics at the local level. But both are still ambulance chasers, targeting drug manufacturers, investment companies, and the medical community, among others.

The major reason ambulance chasers file these lawsuits is to cause enough grief — loss of time and expense — that the person or company being sued will agree to settle. This is known as the Deep Pockets Theory: Once a lawsuit is filed against Mr. Deep Pockets, he will agree to settle at some price rather than go through the legal process — and take the chance of showing just how deep his pockets are.

It's my firm belief that the legal profession is the only profession in America that can legally commit both the conspiracy to extort funds, and actually extort funds, from the public. They do this by filing totally worthless lawsuits solely with the intention to settle or win big cases and bank big bucks from Deep Pockets. The real culprits in the legal profession will do anything — and I mean *anything* — they can get away with.

Since extortion by anyone else is a felony in America, how did we get into this ridiculous situation? The answer is simple: We elected lawyers to political offices and they wrote the laws.

There is one other thing that I want to point out. During the 1960s and 1970s, I was a member of a civil defense unit in Amarillo. I was a volunteer member of the Amarillo Emergency Service. Our group assisted at the scene of many major vehicle accidents.

I can recall pulling several people out of a burning vehicle, and rescuing a lady in a crushed car who was choking. In each case, we were acting before an ambulance arrived. I quit counting the fatal crashes I worked on when the number reached 100.

We volunteers had some protection from liability because of the Good Samaritan Law. Let me say now, that today, with the ambulance-chasing lawyers around, blatantly soliciting lawsuits, I would have serious reservations about doing anything around a wreck. I would not want to be the target of some ambulance-chasing lawyer, because I was trying to save a life in an emergency situation.

These are trying times we are living in, what with the possibility of having contingent liabilities involving perceived violations of civil rights, privacy, etc. A lawsuit can be filed by anyone against anybody and for any reason, whether it has the slightest merit or not.

I could go on and on pointing out ways in which the legal profession is harming America, but suffice it to say, Americans are in a defensive posture in just about everything they do — in business dealings and our personal lives.

Chapter 7

The Tax Code

If a poll were to be taken today in America to determine public opinion of the Federal Tax Code, the result of that poll would be condemnation of the existing system. That opinion would be expressed by all age groups, all political affiliations, and all ethnic backgrounds, all of the groups that the politicians separate us into for their purposes. One might wonder why people of such diverse opinions agree on this one thing.

One doesn't have to be a tax specialist to recognize that the Code is a total nightmare. The perceptions people have of the Tax Code are varied as the people who try to deal with it. Arguments and disagreements occur over those interpretations every minute of the day.

Before even taking a superficial look at the Tax Code, I think it is important to point out a basic reality of federal taxes and any discussion of taxes.

I make this statement with all my heart, for I believe it is absolutely true: The Federal Tax Code is the most powerful political tool in the arsenal of national politicians.

Since political campaigns at the national level are all about dividing people along economic lines, then in order for a federal representative to campaign for election or reelection, he must be in a position to discredit either the candidate of the other party, the federal system, or both. In many cases, pointing out those differences can be informational and positive in nature.

A politician might say the other party is throwing money away on programs that the government should not be involved in. So it is the government's fault for being so wasteful, along with his opponent, who wants those same programs continued or increased. He is saying there is an unfair tax burden on too many people.

His opponent, conversely, says the programs are not getting proper funding because some people have lots of tax breaks, plenty of money, and pay no taxes. Consequently, the poor people are suffering at the hands of the rich, who, he says, pay little or no taxes due to loopholes in the Tax Code.

These two basic allegations never end. They are the essence of national political campaigns, whether for races in the House or the Senate. The real issue is *perception*. Each candidate is the hero, coming to save the people. Neither candidate bothers to mention that both major political parties created the quagmire of legislation over many decades. Without the Tax Code to use as an excuse for all the problems, they would have little to campaign about on a daily basis.

As I said before, we are a divided nation, divided mainly by economics. The pure hypocrisy of attempting to divide people by stressing economic differences is also used to further divide people along racial lines. How many times have we heard a national politician compare the quality of life between various racial groups by pointing out the differences in their economic lives?

Those statements imply that the Tax Code was constructed in some manner to reward the rich at the expense of the poor, and are inflammatory and intentional. The politicians *want to* inflame and blame.

What about statements from the perceived candidate of the rich talking about larger government programs, some of which result in what they call wasteful economic benefits for the poor? Is he really talking about people, or perhaps just wasteful spending?

Many allegations by opposing candidates, or opposing parties, have one common ingredient: The other party is using the Tax Code to put the screws to somebody. Without the Tax Code, federal candidates would have little to campaign about because allocations of the federal budget, obviously generated by the Tax Code, are what campaigns are all about.

Let's talk about the rich and the poor, the haves and the have-nots. What constitutes being poor? What constitutes being rich? Isn't it mostly in the eyes of the beholder?

A person who drives a clunker that sometimes runs and sometimes won't, who is trying to take care of a family of four in a two-room flat, and only has a handful of the most basic foods on hand — is he poor? Most people would probably say "Yes, he is poor."

What about a person who has only the clothes on his back and slept last night in a trash container? These are a couple of examples of one extreme end of the economic ladder.

What constitutes being rich? Is it a person who has a 2,000-square-foot brick home in a manicured neighborhood, owns two or three late-model cars, and eats many meals at nice restaurants?

Perhaps it's the person who lives in that huge estate with the four-car garage, servants' quarters at the back of the lot, totally surrounded by an ornate iron fence that secures the entire acreage.

Perhaps wealth is in the eyes of the beholder, the same as beauty, old age, good luck, or any other subjective variable.

The point to all of this is that America is America. In order for this country to function properly, to remain a land of opportunity, to reward human efforts to succeed and actually have some respect for the free enterprise system, we will have people in every conceivable economic class that exists. That's what America is all about.

Approximately half of all the tax filers in the U.S. pay *no* federal income tax. That is a fact, not my opinion.

Many of them *think* they pay federal income tax, but in reality the dollars withheld are only the federal withholding taxes (Social Security). Due to their income levels, exemptions, and deductions, no federal income tax is paid.

I mentioned in the chapter concerning lawyers the subject of contingent liabilities and taxes on manufacturing facilities. Well, national politicians constantly campaign on the Tax Code, but at the same time constantly seek federal taxes from any conceivable source. Did you know that the United States is *the only country in the world* that taxes all income based on citizenship? Yes, income from anywhere in the world is fully taxable under the U.S. Tax Code, just as though it had been earned in the United States. This is yet another reason why the manufacturing sector in America is fast becoming nothing more than a memory. Faced with sometimes radical labor costs, excessive regulation, ever-increasing class action lawsuits, and even taxation on gains made in other countries, it is no wonder why we are in such a precarious position today.

America has a trade imbalance of 600 billion dollars or more each year. How all this will end is quite predictable. In the future we will see foreign companies not only supplying more consumer items to America, but without any American ownership in them. We are in the process of digging our own economic grave.

A while back, one estimate of the Federal Tax Code was around 16,000 pages. Whether or not that amount has recently increased, one thing is certain: It is unbelievably complex and incredibly expensive for many millions of tax filers to deal with each year.

Just how many accountants, assistants, seasonal tax preparers, comptrollers, treasurers, and so forth can be reasonably required to wade through 16,000 pages? Add all the support personnel in such areas as analysis, posting, preparing reports, and computer related functions and it adds up to a lot of inefficiency.

A common situation in many businesses, both large and

small, is that the overall accounting function, mainly needed to determine and pay federal taxes, is the largest, and perhaps most costly, part of the entire company.

The instruction booklet for calculating 2006 taxes on the IRS 1040 form is an interesting publication. I am certain that thousands of businesses across America would take exception to an item on page 81 entitled, "Estimated Average Taxpayer Burden for Individuals by Activity." A chart shows that 68 percent of all the tax returns in America are filed using the 1040 form and the average total time to complete it is 30.3 hours, costing a mere $269. That includes the completion of "various schedules and accompanying forms."

For the business taxpayer, the total average time allegedly required is 52.2 hours, for a total cost of $470. Let me note this: It is absolutely impossible to file a mountain of various schedules and accompanying forms (as part of the 1040) without spending a vast amount of money in the preparation of data to include on those many forms.

This reminds me of a story I heard in which an absolutely superficial analysis was made in a business venture. The fact that a businessman could buy an item for $5.00 and sell it for $7.00 did not mean he had made a $2.00 "profit" on every sale. That $2.00 was only a margin and there is a world of difference between margin and profit. In reality, he was losing money on every $7.00 sale.

In my business, as in hundreds of thousands of businesses across America, my cost to prepare that 1040 form isn't even close to $470. It is in the many thousands of dollars, due to data collection needed to prepare the various schedules and accompanying forms.

However, consider what large public companies in America have to contend with. With sales in the billions, their complex accounting costs could run into the millions.

One small but expensive point: Every time any change is made in the Code, the greater the costs. Even if incidental, it creates additional labor in the accounting process. And there is no question in my mind that many minor taxes that require only nominal payments by taxpayers cost more to administer than the revenue generated. Still another reason for us to trim those 16,000 pages!

With approximately half of the tax filers in the United States paying no federal income tax, let's take a closer look at the world of reality by analyzing two groups of tax filers: those that pay some level of taxes and those that must file but have no taxes due.

Those people who must file but have no tax to pay are, in all likelihood, paying only federal withholding taxes; they need to still pay something even if they did not earn a large salary because money needs to be put into the system for their retirement, though what they put in may, if they live a long time, be much less than what will be received in monthly checks and medical assistance.

The people who also pay income taxes won't be paying taxes simply on how much money becomes taxable. The basis for their taxes will be on a graduated basis. Plenty of people are of the impression that income taxes are based on some simple rule similar to, "If you make three times as much as I do, you should pay three times more tax than I do."

Nothing could be further from the truth. Let's compare two families, each consisting of a man and wife and three kids; each takes the standard deductions. If one has a taxable income of $50,000 a year and the other's is $100,000, the second family doesn't simply pay twice the income tax. Most people in America are well aware of this, but the national politicians who constantly try to divide people using the Tax Code never bother to mention that the taxable *rate* goes up rapidly on the higher incomes. The politicians also don't bother to tell the vast majority of American tax filers that even their federal withholding taxes are being subsidized by families with higher incomes.

How many times have we heard reports by so-called journalists complaining about how much money some of America's top executives earn? I certainly can't relate to those numbers myself, but what is wrong with putting all that information into context? Just what is proper compensation for a top executive in an American company that has sales in the billions of dollars each year?

An even better question is this: Why does that same announcer/journalist fail to mention the approximate amount of income tax that an executive will pay? Plenty of "poor" people will be subsidized by those dollars. The answer is simple. That reality does not fit the biased opinion of the person delivering the information.

Here is a comparison I can certainly relate to; I invite you to think about this and see if there is a flaw in the analysis.

In the oil and gas business we produce oil and report monthly production in barrels. We sell it by the barrel, pay taxes by the barrel, and pay royalties by the barrel. Everything involving oil wells is computed in barrels. Why is it, then, that if there is ever an oil spill it is measured in *gallons*? The reason is that it shows a bigger number and makes an oil spill sound like a disaster.

There is a constant effort in America to paint capitalism with a broad brush in some fashion, to reflect business in a bad light. There was a time in which America was extremely proud of our nation, our success in manufacturing, and ideas — even promoted freedom and enterprise around the world.

We were also proud as a nation because of the dramatic improvements made in the lifestyles of Americans at all income levels. Case in point: Why do so many people want to come here to improve their lives and, hopefully, achieve the American Dream, while at the same time so many people in America constantly condemn those Americans who have achieved that goal?

Have you ever heard the term "political hypocrisy"? Personally, I want to see as many people as possible, and especially those on the very lowest levels of the income scale, take the time, effort, responsibility, and opportunity to achieve everything possible for themselves.

The American free enterprise system becomes less attractive each year. We simply don't have a universally high regard and respect for the capitalist system. There was a time when there was almost universal support for a system which promised opportunity to those who wanted to pursue it. We as a nation were proud of the accomplishments of others and what the nation's role was in the world.

When I said we will see more countries selling goods to America, and obviously, larger and larger trade deficits, there is no way I could be wrong in that analysis.

There are some very predictable reasons why this situation will get worse. For one, the U.S. is on a spending binge that it can't control. We are doing nothing at all as a nation to actually lessen the scope or cost of government. All we are doing is cutting back on funding for some incidental budget items. Those items are so small they are almost impossible to measure in the total budget.

In the meantime, the really high-dollar items are going through the roof. Congress even had the gall to propose cuts in budget items that wouldn't begin for several years into the future. To propose these strategies, which would become the obligation of a future Congress and a future administration, is so blatantly dishonest it is insulting.

Think about this. The costs of programs such as Medicare, Social Security, health care, and income security require very substantial taxes from current employees and current employers.

Over the years we have seen, and will continue to see, tax rates on income at the maximum. The reason why is quite simple. The U.S. is taxing current employees and employers to the maximum to meet commitments of current programs, including bankrupt programs.

This situation can only get worse. The bottom line is this: The U.S. has made commitments to many millions of people and the programs involved are totally out of control, while the federal representatives continue to use the U.S. Tax Code as their biggest campaign tool.

There are many millions of Americans who want to see a flat tax created to replace our current system. I happen to be one of those that would welcome such a tax program.

But in response to anyone hoping a flat tax will be adopted, forget it. There is no way that a proposal will ever happen. The Federal Tax Code is the vehicle which federal candidates use to perpetuate themselves in office and there is no way they would ever pass a new tax law that would jeopardize their primary means of reelection.

Don't get me wrong about this subject. Many members of the United States House of Representatives and the United States Senate would support a flat tax proposal. The problem is in getting such a proposal submitted and approved. It's not just the political posturing opportunities created by the Tax Code that would block the process, but economic issues of Americans and political pressures *upon* Congress that would kill any momentum.

A *truly* flat tax can never happen, even if a small majority in both the House and Senate wanted to approve it. A so-called flat tax, in its most basic view, is *perceived* as the paying of a certain percentage of income earned. Even if the amount of total income could be reduced by exemptions for the number of people in the family, that would not be acceptable to Americans.

But there can't be a true flat tax if the tax is on income calculated *after* deductions, whether standard or itemized. If tax filers were permitted to itemize deductions in order to reduce the taxable income, the concept of a flat tax system would be a sham; there would be no end to possible deductions. Plus, one issue by itself would drive the nails into the flat tax coffin: interest paid on home loans. An absolutely huge percentage of Americans consider the mortgage interest as their biggest tax break.

People buy homes in order to get this tax advantage, sometimes paying a premium for a home to get the advantage. They enter into mortgages that simply make no sense unless they can garner that advantage, even to the extent of making interest-only loan payments for a period of years or agreeing to variable rate mortgages.

It isn't even necessary to examine the issues involving a flat tax on businesses. We all know that many sophisticated business ventures would fail without some tax benefits. So, if anyone is hoping to ever see a true flat tax in America, they are living in fantasyland. As one of my old Texas buddies used to say, "It ain't gonna happen."

When I discussed the Tax Code in this chapter in 2007, it was the only subject covered. I never anticipated just how bad things could get in the next few years. I knew then that things were bad, but none of us knew what was waiting on the horizon.

Some of those things include:

1. America, through its national so-called leadership, had never gone to such effort to discredit its opposition or opposition's party.
2. We had never heard totally inflammatory personal remarks made about individuals from the floor of the House or Senate relating to tax obligations.
3. Each day there is a constant effort to divide people based upon taxes. It's gotten to the point that if a politician doesn't agree with the other party's position on taxes, that party is a cheat, a criminal or perhaps, isn't faithful to his country.
4. We now find as a public fact that America has the highest corporate tax in the entire world.
5. A current subject of discussion is to find some way to force corporations to move their headquarters back to the United States on the basis that the corporations aren't patriotic. (I should note here that in most cases the reason why corporations moved in the first place was high corporate taxes.)
6. Banking institutions are under fire for activities they were pressured to engage in as the result of

granting loans prior to the housing bust in 2008. Additional compliance rules have created a paperwork jungle for banks. Many banks, especially small ones, have had to close. They couldn't justify the cost of massive regulatory paperwork.

7. The idea of a "flat tax" isn't even worthy of discussion at all today. There's not the slightest chance of it happening.

With all that in mind, let us now go back to December 2012. Remember all the discussion about the "fiscal cliff"? There were budget problems and spending problems facing America, so several weeks prior to December 31, 2012, there were discussions about budget cuts. There was discussion about raising the maximum tax rate from 35 percent to 39.6 percent for anyone having taxable income above $500,000 per year.

The last few days of December 2012 included marathon sessions among politicians. As it turned out, the issue was finally passed to avoid the fiscal cliff late in the evening of December 31. It is quite obvious that nobody really knew what was in that bill. All they knew was that there would be some reductions in the budget and that taxable incomes above $500,000 would be taxed at 39.6 percent rather than 35 percent.

What did we find out within the first week of January 2013? People with taxable income above $200,000 would be subject to the 39.6 percent tax rate. The only budget that was cut was the defense budget.

What did we find out a few weeks later? A lot of people would also be paying 9/10 of one percent to supplement payments into Social Security. They would also be paying 3.8 percent additional taxes on investment income. The 3.8 percent tax would be used to shape up the Social Security Fund.

Let's do a little calculating. Let's say you are wealthy and instead of paying 35 percent, you now pay 35 + 4.6 + .9 + 3.8 for a total tax rate of 44.3 percent. That's an additional 9.3 percent add-on in taxes. Put another way, that 9.3 percent add-on equates to a 26.6 percent tax increase.

I wonder what the responses were of millions of business owners when they found out that they had become targets of a tax that involved them without their knowledge. I will venture to say it made plenty of them change the plans they had for their businesses. These are small businesses. If that weren't bad enough, guess what the effective date was for those new taxes passed during the night of December 31, 2012? You're right, it was the very next day, January 1, 2013. So much for business planning.

Let's put that 26.6 percent tax increase into context. Since it starts when taxable income for the individual hits $200,000, or in the case of a married couple, $250,000, just how would that affect a small business, where the owner reports his business tax obligation when he files his individual tax return? Perhaps the business employs 10-25 people. Why would that business owner be interested in expanding the business, making investments or hiring additional employees simply to pay a lot more in taxes? Why would that business owner be inclined to seek more investment income when facing the highest possible tax rate on each and every dollar of gain?

A question we must all ask ourselves is: If we were one of those business owners trapped by that "fiscal cliff" bill, and it happened once, why would we rule out it ever happening again?

Finally, here's the tax hypocrisy of all hypocrisies. We

as Americans, depending on our taxable income level, in many cases have even lost our standard deduction allowed on the 1040. I am not talking about itemized deductions, but rather a taxpayer simply taking the standard deduction.

Here in the summer of 2014 there's another tax issue being considered. It's so new that it has not been discussed at all, only leaked to the public prior to late July 2014. It now seems that our federal government is concerned about what's being discussed in sermons at some churches. There obviously is distress that politics might be discussed. Where is all of this going?

As I have stated before, the one huge advantage federal government has, through its regulatory agencies, is the Tax Code. We all know now that if groups are of a political persuasion that the leadership of the bureaucracy doesn't like, churches can lose their tax-exempt status, or never have tax-exempt status granted. Are we now at a point in our history that we might be forced to refrain from encouraging people or members of congregations to support needy programs at the local level? Are we supposed to tell our congregations to turn to the government since it obviously knows best what a community needs? In the meantime, since people are more reluctant to make charitable or humanitarian contributions, should tax-exempt status cease to exist for certain churches?

Chapter 8

The News Media

The news media plays a huge role in defining America. Americans and the whole world look to the media in order to determine what we are all about. For hundreds of years everyone was informed at a very slow pace. Even in the 1930s, news traveled slowly.

World War II changed everything. The story of America was spread to the rest of the world, largely in part by our ambassadors in uniform, the military. There was no question that America was a free nation and we were so committed to remaining free that our people were willing to defend freedom around the world.

Even more powerful than the people in uniform, at one point 12 million strong, was the impact of cable television years later. Although cable television in 1965 was unknown, and still in its infancy in 1977, it was starting to reach world viewers even in the early 1970s. Many people in the broadcast industry considered cable a fad that would never affect more than a very small percentage of large population television markets. In fact, during most of that time period, at my station we didn't even consider cable TV a competitor. But everything began to transition into today's market during the late 1970s.

As far as the big broadcast networks in America are concerned, their market is still only the United States, and their share of it continues to shrink. Any outreach to other nations is through their own cable affiliates.

When broadcast television was in its infancy in America, things were quite different from today. Not every family had a TV in their home, certainly not one in each of several rooms in the home, like today.

People watching at retail stores would stand, fascinated. More commonly, people would visit the homes of friends, neighbors, or relatives who owned a TV — perhaps on a regular basis.

In the rest of the world there existed even fewer television sets. It might be a rare occasion for someone to see one at all. After all, the U.S. was one of the few fully developed nations; many countries were rebuilding after wartime destruction or existing as Third World nations.

What the world did see, even if only occasionally, was America's affluence. It had to be quite a shock to millions of people to see just how well Americans lived on a day-to-day basis.

Our standard of living became a topic of discussion around the world, ultimately a believable example of what is possible in a free enterprise democracy. Yet for some, it was viewed with envy or hate.

There was a time when America's news broadcasts simply showed the events of the day. Newscasts were newscasts: Listeners or viewers tuned in to find out about the major events of importance, whether regional, national, or world. There was the occasional commentary by someone in the profession, whether on radio, television, or in the newspaper. But commentaries were always identified as such, with disclaimers for radio or television, or some sort of declarations preceding opinions in the newspaper.

The role played by much of the media has changed dramatically. In many cases, the media *hopes* that the public accepts their messages as simply being reports of news events, while the public is obviously being deceived in many instances. One term often used is "The news behind the news," or something similar, implying that the viewer will get an in-depth look at an event or issue rather than something superficial.

If, in fact, a level of honesty was practiced by news organizations, rather than running promos and constantly referring to their programs as news, some — perhaps all — should say, "News and views." In the years in which I was a television news reporter, and eventually news director, I simply covered the local news. We didn't have a political agenda. That was not why we existed as a news agency.

I will admit that I was interested in politics, but nobody would ever know it. We simply did nothing that was politically slanted. We would sometimes have a slow news day and would develop a story, often human interest in nature, to fill the time. It was never a political story.

During the months leading up to the resignation of President Nixon, I was the Director of News and Public Affairs. In those months of the Watergate investigation, I finally had an opportunity to look at the national media, mostly CBS. I really found out just how vicious and vindictive a news network could be.

The two primary correspondents reporting on White House/Capitol Hill activities for CBS were Roger Mudd and Dan Rather. It was interesting to watch them, especially Dan Rather, as the Watergate story developed from its infancy.

Only rarely did CBS break into normal programming with a news story prior to Watergate. At that time, the networks all but controlled television news in America, since cable was not a serous contender.

Had President Nixon even wanted to go before the American public to admit to his list of crimes and make a sincere apology, the cards were stacked against him. Long before Congress was even discussing the possibility of taking any type of action against the President, the media was in a feeding frenzy. He was tried in the court of public opinion, fashioned by the media, and disgraced; the media was saying he should be impeached even before it was proven that a cover-up was taking place, a cover-up designed to make it appear that crimes took place without the knowledge of the President.

Although the American people can be very understanding and forgiving, the media — like a pack of wild dogs on the hunt smelling red meat — can have their own agenda. I will never forget watching the Roger Mudd and Dan Rather chase. They were not reporting the news, but rather, speculating on what the facts might be while claiming the President should be punished for his wrongdoings.

The network was running numerous bulletins during normal programming. Thanks to their correspondents, especially Rather, the same message was repeated in bulletin after bulletin each day. Rather reminded me of a giddy vulture at a scheduled hanging. Other liberal media jumped on the "Hang Nixon" bandwagon early on, taking about the same approach to the matter.

One evening I announced to the station's news team, writers, and directors, and on the news program to the viewers that the 6:00 p.m. local news program would be local news only and would not include any Watergate coverage. I did that because the local news immediately followed the CBS evening news, and CBS had been airing bulletins continuously for weeks.

The campaign to destroy Nixon was also being conducted by other television news networks, newspapers, and the wire services. But there was little I could do, as a director of news and public affairs, except let the tide run its course.

Another good example of the media's role in politics during the mid 1970s was how one of the wire services helped expedite the departure of one of the administration's cabinet members. At that time the two major wire services were the Associated Press (AP) and United Press International (UPI).

The person who resigned from office was Agriculture Secretary Earl Butz. Secretary Butz was a man who didn't hesitate to give a straight answer to a direct question. As a conservative member who spoke his own mind, he was not warmly received by the liberal media.

Without any notice, Butz resigned from office. There was speculation that some type of scandal might be involved, though not made public. And that if he did not resign, the media was prepared to cause embarrassment to the administration.

Here is what caused the controversy. It seems Mr. Butz was on an airplane sitting next to a popular singer of the 1950s. He related to the singer what could best be described as a joke. It was of a racial nature, and obviously wasn't well received.

At the time Butz was announcing his resignation from office, one of the wire services released the airplane story. I physically tore the paper off the machine and read it myself. There was no question that it would cause embarrassment.

To my knowledge, and certainly I could be wrong, the main incident that caused the resignation was never related to the public. But I found it interesting that even after forcing Butz from office, having won the contest, the wire service couldn't resist trying to smear him.

That was tame compared to today's world of broadcast networks, especially with the cable networks. The Federal Communications Commission has more than a little authority over regular, licensed stations. To show how significant that authority is, we invite the reader to compare some of the *entertainment* shows on cable to those on the broadcast networks.

There is no way that many of the shows on cable could ever appear on the broadcast networks. The FCC wouldn't allow it for a minute. Licenses would be pulled and/or stations would be fined.

How does this laxity affect the cable news programs today? While it is obvious that the broadcast stations are restricted in what they can say and, as most people know, are required to dedicate a certain amount of time to public service broadcasting, the cable stations can do about anything they care to do. There are no standards. Therefore, it is obvious that some people, or stations, will become active participants in the Buffet Syndrome. Their belief is that since there are no standards set for them by the government, they don't need standards.

When stations attempt to present their news programs as being credible, while it is obvious they have a political agenda, it is also obvious that they think the American public is stupid enough that they can't recognize the difference between biased reporting and objective reporting. If, and just if, a cable station actually was concerned about being credible, they should have the decency to admit their agenda to the public and appeal to their substantial party base. At least they would be perceived as honest.

The reader is probably aware of some of the tricks of the trade being used by certain news organizations to disguise their biased reporting. Much of what they do is evident. Some things are just plain sneaky.

Having been employed as a news director, I can say a lot of power rests with the person who determines the content to be included in a news segment. Here are just a few of the things that can be done:

- He (or she) can simply kill a story he doesn't like.
- Create a story which fits his political agenda.
- Submit only one side of a politically sensitive issue.
- Let a guest make a totally baseless charge to inflame public opinion.
- Give substantial time to the side favoring his political opinion while only allowing a token response — perhaps even taken out of context — from the other.

One very effective, and very unfair, tool is to make a comment or allegation at the end of the segment that wasn't even dealt with within the segment. This is done on a regular basis by totally biased news organizations.

As to which technique is used most today to present a

totally biased political agenda, it is the *creation* of a so-called "news story." These stories are designed to influence public opinion or inflame the public.

Obviously, I am very interested in national and world events, and the politics associated with them. I also like to travel to places around the world and see how people in other countries live. My travels and scenic cruises have been eye-opening, perhaps to the point of being educational. I am relating this so the reader will see that I have not lived in a vacuum.

The media in America, especially cable news, allows people in other nations to examine us close-up, sometimes to America's disadvantage. In England, Ireland, Wales, Germany, Austria, Australia, Costa Rica, Honduras, El Salvador, Mexico, the Bahamas, Portugal, Spain, Italy, the Azores, Belize, the U.S. Virgin Islands, Canada, and a few other countries, I found American cable news. In some countries where few television sets are available, people still have occasional opportunities to see America, even in Third World countries.

CNN is available in many countries where no other American broadcast network or cable news network can be seen. That really bothers me. Those foreigners lack what I have at home, where I am able to watch news from many sources.

Whether in another country or on a cruise ship where passengers include people from around the world, what is being presented by American cable news, if only CNN, gives a distorted picture of America. I look around and wonder how so many good people from various nations can still have a positive opinion about America, considering the blatant attempt to paint the values, leadership, and compassion of Americans in such a bad light, especially by CNN.

When I see the daily diatribe of liberal attacks discrediting this nation every day, transmitted to the world by a biased group of henchmen, I simply ask myself these questions: What impressions of America are all these foreigners getting?

Do they think we are starving people by the millions? Do they believe America has a quiet racial war underway at all times? Or that we train our military personnel to commit mass murder around the world?

To Americans, these questions may sound incredibly far-fetched to ask. But based upon the picture being painted by CNN, the Associated Press, *The New York Times,* and others, these insulting questions might be asked by people living in other nations. It is my firm belief that there is a concentrated effort to paint America in the most unfavorable manner possible, for political purposes. With a worldwide audience looking to cable as a national news source, it turns my stomach to see America painted as a bully nation on cable "news" shows as I travel abroad.

We need to face the reality that the views other nations have of America are important in how we deal with the world and our relationships with other governments and peoples. I want to present a problematic scenario, based on my opinions, and ask the reader to supply an answer, or at least think about this.

Let's look at three media organizations in greater detail: *The New York Times*, Associated Press, and CNN — since each of these plays a key role in relating America to Americans and the world.

The New York Times is the dominant supplier of news stories to local and regional newspapers across America. It is also considered the primary newspaper source of American news to many newspapers around the world.

The Associated Press is the wire service that local and regional newspapers across America depend on for many stories, especially events in national political stories from Washington, D.C. It is a rare occasion when a local or regional newspaper does not have several AP stories in an issue.

CNN is in a unique position. In travels to many countries, I have found that CNN was the only American cable news network that could be seen everywhere. Whether in nations where multiple programs are available on TV or on cruise ships, I have found CNN to be available at all times.

The point is this: The three that reach the most people in the world all give absolutely negative views of America in their biased news stories. While never admitting their blatant liberal bias, they constantly attempt to create dissension by painting a negative view of America. It is simply not in their nature to present balanced news.

In the process of carrying out their biased agendas, any political opposition will be discredited, while their organizations' political positions will be embellished. There is an old saying, "You can't win a political argument with the guy who buys ink by the barrel."

The bias at CNN is so blatant that it is insulting. I sometimes watch CNN just to observe their childish efforts to convince people they are credible. They make no attempt to establish even a distorted picture of balance in their presentations. They simply supplement one liberal "news" presenter with another presenter.

If CNN has a guest appear on a political issue, the guest will be as liberal as the program moderator. It is like watching an hourly program each day at the Socialist Party roundtable. One reason CNN bothers me so much is that America has huge economic problems caused by massive social programs, in which there is no funding, and economic collapse is on the way. Rather than having the decency to discuss these problems objectively in the hope that we might start dealing with them, CNN continues to push for more social programs.

They further divide America along economic and racial lines by condemning anyone not supporting their political view. The worst thing about this effort is that they are sometimes the exclusive messenger of America to the world.

For whatever it might be worth, I do have one other thought concerning CNN. I have no idea whether or not I am right in this theory, but here it is. It is my understanding that programming like CNN is sold to various cable service providers for a fee. If that is correct (and it might not be), there are a lot of people who are watching American cable news based upon decisions made by service providers who are seeking the lowest purchase price possible.

If those service providers purchased CNN based solely on the cost of programming, it is understandable why CNN would be selected, rather than paying more for a quality cable news service. I have always heard that you get what you pay for.

Here is a public service announcement from me: I suggest that all of us discuss with friends and business associates the role the media plays — especially the big three — in shaping opinions about America. It just might open up areas of opportunity to change the system.

In the chapter concerning lawyers, remember the discussion about advertisements by lawyers trying to form class-action suits against yet-to-be-named parties in a multitude of industries or environments, supposedly causing some disease or health problem we have never heard of or can't even pronounce? Here's the rest of the story.

WHAT IF I TOLD YOU THAT THOSE ADS CAN RUN AT NO COST? What if I told you that there can be financial gain to the station, or service provider, which in reality makes them a financial partner to that suspect lawyer or law firm?

Law firms are generally prohibited from sharing legal fees with non-lawyers. However, there are companies who can act as intermediary agents between various clients and broadcast facilities. In the advertising contracts, fees are to be paid to a broadcast facility based upon a lead, contact, performance, or per inquiry. In other words, under whatever arrangement put in place by the intermediary company, the broadcast station, network, or service provider can collect compensation for the ads that are running at no cost.

Personally, I think a disclaimer should be provided, showing the relationship between the parties. I find it sickening that we are using the national media to solicit worthless lawsuits to further drive businesses out of the

United States, with stations or service providers actually being parties to this practice.

I will have a suggestion or two in Chapter 10 about how a person can enjoy a little television/newspaper examination on his own, to form his own opinion. I remain, as always, confident that the average American has the intelligence and the ability to make rational judgments.

In 2007 I discussed at length the news organizations, and I think it's important that I update some of those comments, especially as to what I said about CNN. There have been practically no changes in the activities of the Associated Press and the *New York Times*. What has happened in cable news, though, is a completely different matter.

CNN is no longer presenting only one side of an issue. They have lost the contest to see just how totally focused on a liberal agenda that a media channel can be. So it's refreshing to see them pursue, at least on a token basis, a more balanced message to viewers.

It would be interesting to find out if CNN might actually get a few laughs out of another cable news network making fools out of themselves every day, every hour, and every segment.

The really big change in cable news is MSNBC. During the past seven years they have become the most totally disgusting programming source in America. They don't even make the slightest attempt to have any balance in programming. One thing is for sure, you will never see any program on MSNBC that isn't a 100 percent ultra-liberal presentation.

Not one of their anchors, moderators, program hosts or even reporters is anything other than an extremely biased ultra-liberal. There are occasions in which they will run a short statement or picture of someone that they oppose politically. The only reason that's ever done by MSNBC is so that the program moderator can accuse that person of something or give the moderator a podium to express his or her liberal bias.

I do watch MSNBC regularly, but only for a very short period each time. On a consistent basis, nearly all of the program moderators constantly have big smiles on their faces. I guess they are of the opinion that if they smile while delivering their biased baloney, and blasting anyone that doesn't agree with them, America is stupid enough to think they are nice, personable folks.

They remind me of a bunch of adolescents that have the opinion they are entertaining an audience of gullible idiots. What they do have at MSNBC is no credibility.

Chapter 9

Social Security, Medicare, and Other Health Issues

Since America is facing an economic disaster, let us hope our so-called national leaders stop deceiving the nation as to what is really happening with Social Security, Medicare, and other health issues, which are totally out of control and getting worse by the day. Without proper guidance from our national leaders, the chances of avoiding disaster are almost nonexistent.

I have closely followed these issues for many years, and I believe there are no greater examples of citizens participating in the Buffet Syndrome. Here I will point out facts that will show you just how dire the problems are, and encourage you to think *and take action.*

To start with, let's dispel a few common misconceptions about where most of the U.S. taxpayers' money goes. Many people think we give it away to other countries as foreign aid. The truth is that direct foreign aid is an insignificant amount compared to the total federal budget each year.

A common belief is that the huge majority of the budget is used for the military. There's no question that maintaining a military force is expensive, averaging approximately 18 percent of the budget during normal years. Even with a war against terrorism underway, the military budget was still less than 25 percent of the total budget in 2006.

Interest on the national debt is a little above 9 percent, which increases only slightly each year and is a modest increase compared to some other expenditures. As interest rates begin moving up, thanks to some huge unfunded liabilities that have been created in the past two years, interest on the national debt will become a more significant part of the federal budget. The only way that will *not* happen is if taxes go up.

Now for some really big numbers on Health, Medicare, and Social Security. I refer the reader to page 632 of the *2004 Time Almanac,* where you can read these scary numbers.

America spent 172 billion dollars for what is classified as "Health" in the year 2001. The 2006 estimate is 297 billion dollars. Over a five-year period that is a *72 percent* increase.

In 2001, the Medicare program budget was 217 billion dollars. The 2006 estimate is 281 billion. That is a 29+ percent increase.

The budget for Social Security in 2001 was 433 billion compared to the 2006 estimate of 546 billion, or, a 23+ percent increase. The truth is that the *accounting* for Social Security receipts and expenditures is bogus. I will explain later.

Next, I will demonstrate that these three items, along with one titled "Income Security," whatever that is, will, in all probability, cause the United States dollar to be devalued to the point of having little real purchasing power. That is a pretty bold statement, but when all is put into proper context, almost anyone can see why I arrived at that conclusion.

The four budget items, based upon the 2006 estimates, equal almost 1.5 trillion dollars, or *62 percent* of the entire federal budget, *and* growing every day.

Please bear in mind that the total federal budget for 2006 is estimated at 2.4 trillion dollars. There is no question, though, that we have a war underway, are spending even more, and running a big deficit. A huge transition is taking place in America, for it has become difficult to even comprehend the reality of where this nation is as it relates to financial well-being.

The budget item with the largest increase in cost, 72 percent, is health; all efforts to control expenditures have totally disappeared. Although some national politicians brag about what great accomplishments have been made by Washington in getting people off welfare, warming the heart of any listener, it is pure baloney. If the same number of people are qualifying for programs but only *a percentage* are being classified as being on welfare, no positive effect has been made on the reduction of welfare costs.

The hypocrisy of this creative restructuring is that although the nation has been raising the amount of maximum earnings allowed to qualify people for programs, there was supposedly a huge, and I mean *huge decrease* in the number of families on the welfare rolls between 1993 and 2000. What really happened is that most of the families supposedly no longer on welfare simply qualified for benefits from programs *without* being classified as welfare recipients. So any claim of a decrease is totally without merit.

Allow me to put it another way. Let's just say, hypothetically, that 10 million people are below the poverty level. All 10 million would qualify for welfare benefits of some sort. Let's say the next 10 million above that income level are, obviously, not below the poverty level. As such, that next 10 million would not qualify for welfare programs as they are above the poverty level. That sounds reasonable, doesn't it? As it turns out, things are not always as they seem.

What is really happening in America today is that the federal bureaucracy is qualifying people by the millions for welfare programs even though they have incomes well above the poverty level. It's just a program name change, a shell game.

These programs become more and more expensive each year as more and more people, whose earnings are well above the poverty level and should not qualify for welfare programs, become more and more dependent upon the taxpayers for more and more financial support. And it gets worse each year.

I want to take this opportunity to ask the reader a simple question: If your government was making every effort possible to qualify you for every freebie program available, all of which came to you with no tax consequences, to the point that you can live a better lifestyle than working at a low-paying job, would you even want to look for a job?

Look again at the 72 percent increase in the health budget. That increase was caused mainly by people qualifying for health services, even though they might have incomes above the poverty level and were not on the welfare rolls.

What we have are people utilizing the system in every way possible. In other words, if a program can be utilized without cost to a citizen, he takes it. The Buffet Syndrome strikes again.

What makes all this especially bad is that as people find more and more programs to sign up for if they can qualify, there is more motivation for them to achieve less and less on their own, perhaps to the point of wanting to accomplish nothing, thereby insuring the maximum amount of freebies. Many programs can be qualified for even if wages are being received.

Since the ever-increasing trend is for programs mandated at the federal level to be the financial responsibility of state and local governments, there is no true guess as to what the real expenditures of some of these federal programs would be if, in fact, federal tax dollars were actually doing all the funding.

We come now to my favorite two budget items, Social Security and Medicare, which by themselves have the ability to throw the dollar and our economy into total disarray. It is almost impossible to separate them since they each have such monumental structural and actuarial similarities and problems. I will also incorporate the prescription drug plan into the mix.

Here is where history and statistics are vitally important in understanding where we are headed.

In 1940, *the average life expectancy for a man in America was 60.8 years. For a woman, 65.2.* When Social Security began in 1935, it was estimated that *only 1 in 50 people would ever draw Social Security retirement benefits.* That makes sense, especially considering that most of the workforce was men. Times have changed dramatically.

In the year 2000, *the average life expectancy for a man was 74.1 years and 79.5 for a female.* These are radical increases in life expectancy.

Over the years, changes have been made to the guidelines of Social Security to create additional guarantees of security to recipients and their families. Since Americans are *not* big believers in saving money for retirement, the role of Social Security over the years has changed. Once viewed as a supplementary income to savings or retirement, for many millions of Americans — more than we even want to think about — Social Security is the *only income* they have to live on. These are not isolated situations at all. In fact, it is very common across America for people drawing Social Security to have no other supplemental income or savings, yet still pay rent.

The votes placed by senior citizens can easily determine the outcome of any federal election. With an estimated 49 million persons currently drawing Social Security retirement, and the fact that many of those millions have nothing else, we have a problem.

When I turn to page 758 of the *2001 World Almanac and Book of Facts*, I read these words:

> *It Is a Fact.* Today there are 3.4 workers paying Social Security for each person receiving benefits. By 2030, there will be only 2.0. On the basis of current provisions, incoming revenue will fall short of covering the benefits around 2012. Trust Fund reserves would make up the difference for a period of time after that.

Since that publication date, especially in the last three

years, I have heard shortfall estimates ranging from 2012 to as late as 2018. But nothing beyond.

Here is the biggest bombshell of all: No topic in America's history has been so totally misrepresented as the so-called Social Security Trust Fund. To be blunt: THERE IS NO TRUST FUND, THERE HAS NEVER BEEN A TRUST FUND, AND THERE NEVER WILL BE A TRUST FUND. The truth is that millions of people in America know that, but they simply can't face reality.

There isn't one single member of the House or Senate, at least for the past 12 years, who doesn't know there is not a Trust Fund. They still allow the subject to be discussed and say nothing about the true facts.

We have current contributions and current expenditures in the Social Security program, much like a business has current revenues and current expenses. Ideally, we need 90 days of revenues in Social Security contributions above expenditures. As a general rule, contributions of 60 days are on hand, over and above the current month's expenditures. The administration really gets concerned if the reserves fall below 45 days to cover expenses.

The Trust Fund is nothing but a sham. It doesn't exist, and the American people have been deceived, for far too long. We are living longer and a smaller percentage of people are paying into the system. Those are the facts.

If a corporation in America presented a report to the Securities Exchange Commission and to their shareholders, based upon the practices being used to report on the so-called Social Security Trust Fund, the stockholders could sue them for misrepresentation and fraud — and win! The Securities Exchange Commission could institute action to the Justice Department to try the officers of the corporation and send them to prison.

The so-called Trust Fund, believe it or not, is showing an increase each year. *There are no funds.* There are only IOUs — U.S. Bonds — issued by the government and payable by the taxpayers. They have the gall to show *interest income* coming to the Fund, which supposedly creates the annual increase.

The interest being shown as *income* is really interest owed by the taxpayers on the IOUs that were issued. Those IOUs (bonds that are part of the federal debt) are a *liability*, not an asset. Let corporate America show liabilities as assets and they are in deep trouble.

The following is absolutely the most important part of this book. Your political affiliation makes no difference. Whether you are a Democrat, Republican, have no affiliation at all, or are part of a radical fringe element to the left or right — and no matter what your age might be — the bottom line to the following scenario is the same, so please think about this.

Many people believe Social Security was plundered by either Republicans or Democrats. Some think it went into the general tax fund and was spent. Some think bonds have been issued and there is a vast Trust Fund just sitting there. Others think it was used to support the military or other programs. EVERYBODY HAS AN OPINION OF WHAT HAPPENED TO ALL THE MONEY THAT WAS SUPPOSED TO GO TO SOCIAL SECURITY.

In the final analysis: ALTHOUGH THERE IS NO TRUST FUND AND THERE HAS NEVER BEEN ONE, SOME 100 MILLION PEOPLE HAVE PLANNED THEIR LIVES AROUND IT AND SOME 49 MILLION PEOPLE ARE CURRENTLY DRAWING SOCIAL SECURITY.

However, one positive note that is welcome information to people either drawing retirement or planning for it in the near future is that the amount of the retirement check will be not be reduced. If a person is getting $900 a month now, they will definitely not get a lesser amount per month in the future.

The reasoning is simple. If a vote was taken in the House or Senate to reduce the monthly check, every member who voted for a reduction would be defeated at the next election. It wouldn't matter which party they were in or their seniority;

that one vote would end their political career.

President Bush found out just how politically charged the subject of Social Security could be when he tried to present the problem to the American public. For many years I hoped that one President would have the guts to tell the truth about the terrible financial position of Social Security. We went through Republican and Democratic administrations alike without the subject being discussed at all.

President Bush's ill-fated venture into the subject was made so recently that I suspect most Americans remember what happened. The effort took him to quite a few cities in America, a different city each day for a week, but he might as well have stayed in Washington. In fact, he might as well have been given a shovel to help dig his own grave.

He wasn't just confronted with differing opinions. He was systematically demonized from various groups, politicians, and in particular, the media. There was a national effort, which also included the AARP, to accuse him of robbing the *so-called* Trust Fund.

Wherever he went to relate his concerns, he was literally stiffed. His message went absolutely nowhere — in many ways, thanks to the media.

We have all heard of politicians having to navigate through a mine field, but in this case it was more like avoiding the triggering device for an atomic bomb. It is ironic that so much was done to destroy a President accused of "robbing the Trust Fund," when in reality there was nothing to rob, even if he had wanted to. What he wanted to do, and did, was tell the truth.

Although Social Security is bankrupt and has always been actuarially defunct, Americans have been promised income security. Social Security wasn't even designed to be actuarially sound. It was never conceived to be a supplementary retirement program to redistribute monies to participants with an extended period of low income.

There is a huge disparity between the lowest monthly check paid and the highest monthly check. A person with high earnings for an extended period of time is rewarded upon retirement with only a nominal check, compared to the amount paid into the system.

In the meantime, many people look to this program, which is an *entitlement* program, actuarially unsound from the beginning and bankrupt, as an *absolute right*.

Let's move now to Medicare, the final subject of this chapter. The costs of this program are almost too large to calculate. Medical costs represent more than 17 percent of the Gross National Product and the percentage is increasing each year.

Remember those life expectancy figures I cited as part of the discussion of Social Security? They are even more important when medical costs are being discussed. As people continue to live longer, the costs for medical services become incredibly high. There are so many reasons why Medicare has disaster written all over it.

First, there is nothing to stop the trend of increasing costs of the program. We have *at least* 49 million people on the program, and they are living longer than ever before.

Second, extremely professional people are as guilty as, or probably guiltier, of engaging in the Buffet Syndrome than any other sector of society. Whenever a vast federal program can be expanded, they get very creative. The Medicare program has spawned business opportunities that its founders never dreamed of.

I have already pointed out just how much this program is costing the American taxpayers each year, and it is growing at an alarming rate. Let's cut to the meat of the issue and discuss a couple of the realities of life.

Many people on Medicare are of the opinion that the deductions made from their Social Security checks as a Medicare premium actually pay the costs of the health services they are receiving. They actually believe it is like a health insurance premium paid to a private health insurance company, except they pay Medicare. The truth is that the extremely small deductions from their checks *don't even come close* to paying for the services being rendered.

The American taxpayer, currently employed and paying federal income taxes, is the person paying nearly all the costs of the Medicare program. If the truth was known, and most people on Medicare were forced to pay realistic premiums for services rendered, they would pay many hundreds of dollars per month, *at a minimum*.

It's important that everyone understands just how severe the problem of financing Medicare will become. It's already a nightmare, but will eventually become a full-fledged American disaster, and there are several valid reasons why this is, in fact, going to happen. I am even going to show them in numerical order. Please stay with me on this because this is important.

1. We have a huge population above age 65.
2. There are absolutely no reserves to fund Medicare.
3. People still working and earning incomes are paying almost all the current costs of the Medicare program.
4. Current Social Security retirees' "contributions" to Medicare each month are almost nothing.
5. Technology and new medical procedures are unbelievably expensive, and there are new technologies and new procedures being administered constantly.
6. Our older population continues to live longer, and absorb even higher costs for even longer periods of time.
7. Many medical procedures performed are, in reality, elective procedures.
8. None of the "contributions" paid in today by hardworking employees and business owners have even the remotest possibility of being around for their own future benefit.

The second reality that we all must face concerns the medical community and the extremely professional people who make up that community, including doctors and hospitals. In the final analysis, no matter how many degrees a person might have, in whatever specialty, he is still a businessman, and in this case, his business is medical services. So too is any medical facility, be it a clinic, hospital, or something else.

I find in some Sunday newspapers here in Amarillo a full-page ad by one or both of the two major hospitals. They are businesses, so they advertise to get business. I often also see advertising by other medical providers, including doctors.

It's important that you be aware that the events I am about to relate to you are firsthand knowledge, not opinion or speculation. Typical of a person with a serious health problem over an extended period of time, I have had a lot of unforgettable experiences.

Nearly nine years ago I had a heart attack. My first medical bills totaled more than $77,000, including a quadruple bypass, followed by a procedure to correct my heart's conduction system. I don't recall what the cost was for that one.

The third procedure involved placing two stents in my heart. I will elaborate more on that procedure and related costs. I then had a heart catheterization, followed by a second operation to have two additional stents placed in my heart. This will be the second procedure for which I will itemize the charges.

So here I am today with four bypasses, four stents, and one artery still plugged and inoperable. All the while, having at least three events in my life which could easily have killed me, and I'm still a walking time bomb.

I have been involved in heart health problems as a privately insured patient and later as a Medicare patient. Regardless of what status a patient might have, one thing is sure: Somebody, whether an insurance company or Medicare, is about to get some huge bills to pay.

I recall after my heart bypass surgery that I was given a small plastic item that looked like a cheap toy. It had a plastic ball in a tube. I had to blow in it to help build up the strength in my chest and lungs. It looked pretty simple and junky, though I admit it might have had $5.00 in materials in it. My hospital bill showed what my insurance company had been billed for that contraption and had paid $3,000.

Now for some firsthand information about the hospital business. For the initial hospital stay where I had two stents placed in my heart, the bill from the specialty clinic that did the surgery was for several thousand dollars and that came as no surprise.

What came a week later was a real shocker. I went into the hospital at 1:00 p.m. one day, had the surgery that afternoon, stayed overnight, and then went home at 11:00 a.m. the next day. So, I spent less than 24 hours in the building. The bill was for nothing except hospital charges in support of the surgeon, who had billed separately. According to this statement, more than $13,700 was paid by Medicare to the hospital!

The statement went on to say that there was the possibly some $900 more in hospital charges that Medicare did not pay that I might have to donate. Fortunately, my supplemental policy covered them.

Think about it: $13,700 for 22 hours in the hospital, without any doctors' costs included, would be a full year's salary for a person being paid $6.50 per hour and working all 52 weeks in a year.

Have you ever heard the term "creative billing"? I have examined some of the charges submitted to Medicare and they are hard to believe. It would appear that a simple charge, for example, might appear as several entries rather than a single amount, all with a different coding as to what it was, and with an additional cost for each coded entry. A visit to any medical facility by a person on Social Security and Medicare is quite an experience. In the final analysis, what you have is simply a customer going into a business.

When most businesses advertise an expensive product or service, the price involved is always a major consideration to the shopper. Well, *almost* always, that is. When was the last time any price was included in an advertisement for medical services? When was a patient given a summary of anticipated charges for a surgical procedure? When was the last time a chart was hung in a doctor's office showing the prices for even routine things like a blood test, office call, EKG, or vaccination?

Doctors and hospitals, as a general rule, set their own prices and don't even think about telling anyone what they are. It is interesting to me that a dentist can tell someone what it will cost to pull a tooth, put in a filling, or even do an extensive surgery, while an assistant in a doctor's office uses a different approach. How can a nursing assistant doing five minutes of work, *or less,* in running an EKG, cost $85? Without even asking me! I haven't been in a heart facility in the past 10 years where I was asked if I wanted an EKG.

It strikes me that the medical facilities are really having a field day, especially hospitals. Since most people never see the hospital bill, as it goes directly to Medicare for payment, they have no idea just how extensive the padding of the bill can be. How can a hospital justify charging $7.00 for a single aspirin? One hospital did.

There is no question that having to deal with a massive bureaucracy in a complicated program such as Medicare causes costs to increase dramatically. In defense of the medical community, it must be a nightmare, requiring *considerable* additional staffing to support the mountains of paperwork. So the costs of medical services continue to spiral upwards in large part due to the bureaucratic quagmire mixing into the health care system.

All of us are thankful that people are living longer because of the innovations in the medical community. As recently as the World War II years, our elderly population quite often died of what was referred to as "old age." People don't die from old age today; they die from specific medical problems. As our people grow older and their bodies tend to start developing problems, America has some truly amazing tools at its disposal to deal with almost any situation. Doctors can diagnose almost anything, and then treat it, correct it, or even replace a body part that is wearing out.

However, for many people, after months or years of dealing with health problems, at some point there is nothing more that can be done. It is then that the medical community simply tries to prolong the life of a person for as long as possible. Please don't think I am implying that a life should be ended at some point. All I am saying is that usually there is a huge expense in maintaining a life.

This is something to think about. There will be plenty of opportunities for creative billing if it is standard procedure to do everything that could *possibly* be done. Medicare is aware, and will only pay certain amounts for certain items. So the battle rages every day because many are engaging in the Buffet Syndrome medical style, trying for everything they just *might* get, or get some *portion of.*

To prove how creative they can get, I have the bill from my most recent hospital stay, when the second set of stents was placed in my heart. Be careful. This is hard to believe, and it would be the subject for a book of fiction, were it not so absolutely and financially true.

My bill from an Amarillo hospital was for services performed over two days. This bill, dated August 27, 2007, was a recap by my insurance company for two more stents placed in my heart.

This is for hospital charges only and does not include the heart facility and the surgeon who performed the service. That charge was $10,710.00.

When I saw the charges billed to my health service provider I couldn't believe it. The total was $33,570.75, reflecting a room charge of one day! Talk about creative billing!

I took the insurance company recap and went to the hospital to get a copy of the actual bill from the hospital. As you might know, most of us sign documents which allow hospitals to bill the health insurance provider service directly so that few people ever see the hospital bills themselves. I have mine in hand now and here are some of the things on it. The two stents, $6,637.50 each. The two EKG's, which take about five minutes each, were $127.50 each. The total bill from the hospital, which included thousands of dollars in equipment used in the procedures, was $33,614.75, of which my health care provider paid $33,570.75.

The medicines really tell the story of creative billing. Have you ever heard the term healthy mark-up? That's normally used when a retail facility charges more than a reasonable mark-up above its cost for an item. It's also sometimes referred to as "a percentage mark-up, and then some."

I want to show you what was done in pricing nine drugs/vitamins I was given during my 32-1/2 hours at the hospital. You will see how much each pill was billed for by the hospital compared to what my neighborhood pharmacy charges for a 30-day supply. I then show how much each of them charge for one pill. The last figure is the percentage of mark-up comparing the hospital's fee to the pharmacy price.

ITEM	COST PER PILL	MARK-UP
Hospital Clopidogrel 75 mg. (Plavix)	$33.51	
Pharmacy, for 30, $137.99	4.593	629.59%
Hospital Ezgtimibe 10 mg (Zetia)	16.59	
Pharmacy, for 30, 102.85	3.4283	384.38%
Hospital Feno Fibrate 145 mg (Tricor)	20.74	
Pharmacy, for 30, 121.38	4.046	412.61%

Hospital		
AMLodipine 10 mg	16.93	
Pharmacy, for 30, 28.66	.9553	1,672.22%
Hospital		
Vitamin E 400 Unit	1.16	
Pharmacy, for 30, 10.82	.09016	1,186.60%
Hospital		
Multi-Vitamin-T	1.16	
Pharmacy, for 365, 9.52	.02608	4,347.85%
Hospital		
Toprol XL 50 mg	29.79	
Pharmacy, for 30 —		
substituted generic		
Metoprolol XL		
50 mg 23.54	.7846	3,696.84%
Hospital		
Imdur SR 60 mg	17.07	
Pharmacy, for 30 —		
substituted generic		
Isosorbide 8.91	.297	5,647.47%
Hospital		
Simvastatin 20 mg	32.96	
Pharmacy, for 30 —		
substituted		
H generic 13.56	.452 7	192.04%

I'm reasonably sure that a large hospital doesn't pay more for prescription medicines and vitamins than my neighborhood pharmacy, so there is no way that I could ever be convinced that creative billing had *not* taken place. It's no wonder that medical costs in America represent such a huge percentage of the Gross National Product, and unfortunately, are only getting to be a larger problem as time goes by.

I was also billed for one children's aspirin. The cost —

only 4 cents. This tells me one thing. Someone has called them out before on creative billing and it is hard to hide something as simple as the best-known medicine in America — aspirin. No telling what the cost would have been if that aspirin could have had a different name. Creative billing is alive and well.

If the truth was known, every person on Medicare who walks into a medical facility is viewed as a cash cow, might as well have dollar signs tattooed on their foreheads, signals that all types of revenue streams are forthcoming, thanks to American taxpayers. When a business goes up for sale, in most cases, "Blue Sky" makes up a significant part of the value of the business. That is, client lists, persons using the company's products, good credit customers, and potential clients all add value. People on Medicare are often viewed as limitless walking billing machines.

There is another side to the story of that relationship between the Medicare recipient and others. In this case, let's defend the facility about to deliver medical services.

Let's just say, hypothetically, that a person on Medicare has a hip that bothers him a bit. He is perhaps in his 70s and doesn't work. He can move around pretty well, but not as well as he did 20 years ago. He has heard about a new procedure to make that hip as good as new. Bearing in mind that having an operation will not radically disrupt his life and Medicare will pay for the procedure and hospital costs associated with it, what will he do? He will try to get it done. The reader probably knows someone who has been in this position, which in reality is a type of *elective* surgery.

It is the classic example of all examples of the Buffet Syndrome. If he had to pay $100 for a single office call *out of his pocket,* to be referred to the surgery, he would probably get angry. For a procedure that might cost American taxpayers 50 to 75 thousand dollars. YET HE PROBABLY WILL NEVER EVEN ASK WHAT THE COSTS WOULD HAVE BEEN, AND HE COULDN'T CARE LESS.

The Buffet Syndrome strikes again!

Chapter 10

Other Thoughts, and What Is the Answer to the Buffet Syndrome?

As I stated previously, the most important part of this book is the previous chapter on Social Security and Medicare. Closely related to them are the prescription drug plan and health care in general. As chance would have it, that chapter became one of the largest chapters in the book and I needed more incidents to sum up my conclusions, so I allowed the prescription drug plan to overflow into this chapter.

I present three incidents that occurred near the end of my work on this book. Talk about timely!

I related earlier how the standard practice of running an EKG takes less than five minutes and costs $85. Well, the last time I was tested I was told there would be a new test to check the circulation of blood in the feet and ankles. The nursing assistant told me that every patient would be tested *at least* once a year.

Sure enough, when I went back in I was hooked up. It was almost comical to observe the contraption, which bounced sounds around the room like an amplifier on a bubble machine. The test took less than 10 minutes and I can hardly wait to see how many hundreds, or thousands, of dollars the charge will be.

I was reminded of an incident many years ago where a buddy of mine had built a console for dispatching radio transmissions to mobile units; he was trying to sell the console to a company. It had one row of red lights that would turn on and off every few seconds. I asked him what purpose the light display served and he told me, on a confidential basis, that it would help seal the deal. In other words, it looked impressive, served no purpose, but would likely put money in his pocket. Was that console the predecessor to today's bubble machine in stereo?

Incident number two: This week my wife received a letter from the Social Security Administration concerning the Medicare prescription drug program. The letter started like this: "You may be eligible to get extra help paying for your prescription drugs." Another example of the requirement to notify people when any federal entitlement program is created, either by notification from governors' offices in various states or regional planning commissions — notifications that can actually be *solicitations* to people to participate, whether they need to be told or not.

Bear in mind that the nation has already been thoroughly notified of the Medicare prescription drug program, which began January 1, 2006. The *unsolicited* letter to my wife was in fact an attempt to qualify her for extra help in paying for drug expenses.

The seven-page document, of which five were in the form of a questionnaire, was, in my mind, prepared *to entice a* person to attempt to qualify for benefits. There was no objectivity in the form.

The Medicare prescription drug program, in reality, will wind up being the drug plan for all Medicare recipients, and, more importantly, the nation's *Medicaid* prescription drug program, with both absorbed into our defunct Social Security program.

We were sold a bill of goods when the prescription drug program was created. We were told the program would cost some 500 billion dollars over a 10-year period. We were not told that Medicaid costs would merge into that program and subsequently become part of the Social Security financial disaster, hastening its collapse.

We were not told that the forms to sign up for the program would not only enroll people in the new drug program, but *encourage* people to try to qualify as though they had previously been on Medicaid. *Medicaid is not part of Social Security.* Again, *solicited* participation in entitlement programs is a detriment to all programs and a burden on the American taxpayer.

Incident number three adds credence to all I have said about the bureaucracy, our national political system, and the Buffet Syndrome — and hopefully encourages all my readers to think for themselves. What I am about to relate was a front-page story in a national newspaper, though I have seen nothing since then. To my knowledge, the information was not picked up in any other newspaper, nor television or radio network.

On Thursday, August 3, 2006, *USA Today* featured this story on the front page and filled up over half of page 2: "What Is the Real Federal Deficit?" A graph showed the official 2005 federal deficit of 318 billion dollars. A second graph reflected a 760 billion dollar deficit, the "Audited Version." A third graph was referred to as the "corporate style" and showed a 2005 deficit of 3.5 *trillion* dollars.

Obviously a *radical* difference, with the last figure 11 times larger than the first. How can there be such a huge difference? Well, the first came from the White House and Congress. The next, the audited version from the Treasury Department. The third graph was based on accounting rules used by corporations *and includes the costs of Social Security and Medicare.*

Interesting that the deficit more than doubles simply because the audited version includes the retirement costs of civil servants and military personnel, but *not* the costs of Social Security and Medicare. Lucky for Congress and the Treasury Department that they are not bound by corporate rules.

The accounting rules that the federal system requires

public companies to use are based on the accrual method. When long-term obligations are created by a corporation, like retirement programs, all liabilities must be recorded on the filings with the SEC, the Securities and Exchange Commission. The federal government does not require itself to include Social Security, Medicare, or the prescription drug plan in its liabilities — as if they didn't even exist, are not part of the nation's public debt. That realistic shortfall of 3.5 trillion dollars is nearly one-third of the entire Gross National Product of the United States in 2005.

The article in *USA Today* was the most informational and compelling article I have ever seen concerning the subject of Social Security, Medicare, and now, the Medicare prescription drug plan. Talk about keeping a fraudulent set of books — this is it.

In the discussion about mandating the federal government to be required to use the same accrual accounting procedures it requires from corporate America, here are a few paragraphs cited from the newspaper:

> The proposal to add Social Security and Medicare to the bottom line has deeply divided the federal accounting board, composed of government officials and "public" members, who are accounting experts from outside government.

> The four government members, who represent the President, Congress and the Government Accounting Office, oppose the change. The retirement programs do *"not represent a legal obligation because Congress has the authority to increase or reduce Social Security benefits at any time,"* wrote Clay Johnson III, then Acting Director of the President's Office of Management and Budget, in a letter to the board in May. (My italics)

The article confirms my opinion that national politicians are hiding from the truth concerning the reality of Social Security and Medicare. Here comes the best part, though. I want to tell you the definition of "actuary" according to *Webster's Universal College Dictionary*, 1997: "Actuary – A person who computes insurance premium rates, dividends, risks, etc., based on statistical data."

In other words, he is the guy who is charged with the responsibility of analyzing a situation based upon the facts, those being premium rates, dividends, risks, and statistical data. This newspaper had an interesting quote from the person who, in his official capacity with the Social Security Administration, knows the most about the financial position of Social Security. I again cite paragraphs from the newspaper article:

> Social Security *Chief Actuary* Stephen Goss says it would be a mistake to apply accrual accounting to Social Security and Medicare. *"These programs are not pensions or legally binding federal obligations, although many people view them that way,"* he says.
>
> "Social Security and Medicare are pay-as-you-go programs and *should be treated like food stamps and fighter jets, not like a treasury bond that must be repaid in the future,"* he adds.
>
> "A country doesn't record a liability every time a kid is born to reflect the cost of providing that baby with a K-12 education one day," Goss says. (My italics)

Just a side note here: You will find that it's not the federal government that provides education for kids starting with kindergarten through grade 12. *State* taxpayers pay almost all of those costs. The truth is that federal "contributions" to our state schools (our tax dollars) are insignificant in the budgets of schools across the country.

That brings to mind another question, just begging for an honest answer. The article also states a treasury bond must be repaid in the future. While it's true that anyone who owns treasury bonds can turn them in for cash, how does the government repay? That's simple. More bonds are issued and the outstanding debt of the nation continues to increase. America is knee-deep in debt and those obligations don't even show up in the budget, as in the case of Social Security obligations, Medicare obligations and yes, the new obligations of the Medicare prescription drug plan.

This same article does an excellent job of putting this new national obligation into context by citing the following:

> The new Medicare prescription drug benefit alone would have added $8 trillion to the government's audited deficit. That's the amount the government would need today, to pay for the *tens of trillions* of dollars the benefit will cost in future years.
>
> Standard accounting concepts say that $8 trillion should be reported as an expense. Combined with other new liabilities and operating losses, the government would have reported an *$11 trillion deficit in 2004* — about the size of the nation's entire economy. (My italics)

Again, that deficit *should* have been reported. After all, why shouldn't our federal government, which requires all of corporate America to use the accrual process for reporting liabilities, be subject to the same guidelines itself? Now if that wasn't hypocrisy in action based upon the single year of 2004, here is what was done just four years prior. I'm again citing directly from the article:

> The federal government also would have had a *$12.7 trillion deficit* in 2000 because that was the first year that Social Security and Medicare reported broader measures of the *programs unfunded liabilities.* That created a one-time expense. I might add here that I have no idea what those "programs unfunded liabilities" might have consisted of. One thing's sure though. They, in only one year, suddenly discovered liabilities in an amount more than all the reported debt ever created in the entire history of this country. (My italics)

Although, supposedly, the national debt of the United States is below 10 trillion dollars, an amount amassed during our entire history as a nation, these two items alone, if honestly reported to the nation, would have more than tripled the national debt.

I will have something else to add to this topic in the next chapter. I will give various scenarios about some things, and in each case, will be seriously asking you to consider these important issues and form your opinion.

The Bush Administration opposed including Social Security and Medicare in the audited deficit. Their reasoning: Congress can cancel or cut the retirement programs at any time, so they should not be considered a government liability for accounting purposes. However, what would happen if a cut was published in every newspaper and sent out on all television and radio networks in America?

Imagine the outcry from the 49 million people currently on Social Security retirement and Medicare, who would be demonstrating in the streets and contacting their federal officials on a daily basis. The AARP would run radio, television, and newspaper ads vilifying the Administration. The 100 million or so citizens who are planning their futures around it would be alarmed. Practically every Democratic House member and senator would be jumping in front of the cameras to condemn the present administration, going on all the talk radio programs to express their outrage, even introducing legislation to censure or impeach the President.

Why is none of this happening? The answer is quite simple: All the politicians in recent history are guilty of letting the charade continue. They will never publicly criticize themselves. But they *will* try to shift the blame to their opposition, *whoever* the opposition is at any one time.

Why is the public not in an uproar? Most Americans know we have been burying our heads in the sand, hoping that an economic catastrophe *won't come in our lifetimes.* Why haven't we had the decency and honesty to deal with a problem we know can easily bankrupt America? I sincerely hope we wake up.

For whatever it might be worth, I have been concerned for many years about leaving these massive financial problems, still not dealt with, to my family and future Americans. The position we are leaving to our young people is, in my opinion, nothing short of criminal.

The vast majority of American families are honest hard-working people, proud of their nation, the state they live in, and their local communities. They should be proud of themselves and our nation. Our ability to deal with adversity is amazing.

But we need to place a lot more trust in the qualities of the people who are actually making the system work. And our leaders must get the message across that our productivity is not a buffet, a crop to be harvested. The national goal should not be to harvest the largest crop, the largest percentage of tax revenues, or the GNP.

If the people become a buffet, a crop to be harvested, we are simply the target behind the federal manure spreader.

The key to dealing with massive economic problems is this: *Americans must be given the true facts.* The days of withholding information, distorting others, and simply playing the blame game must come to an end. It makes no sense to continue a process that is only guaranteed to get worse each year. In other words, be honest with us regarding real problems.

I just wish the government had as much confidence in the huge majority of the American people as I do, and as most of us have in ourselves.

Finally, I would like to recommend a few actions we might all consider doing, because every citizen must take the responsibility to plan for the future and not depend on anyone else. And know what is happening in the country, since the federal system has lost all interest in correcting itself. I am passing along techniques I have successfully used to radically enhance my future.

As I stated previously, America is a nation of consumers. Since the 1950s, we have gone from being a country that manufactures items to sell to ourselves and the world to mainly a service industry economy. A huge segment of America's families are servers and consumers of everything imaginable. We are constantly besieged with advertising that says we must buy, buy, and buy. When one considers the vast amount of hours most Americans spend parked in front of the television set, it is obvious that America creates the top marketing professionals in the world.

We not only buy things we really don't need, but things we really can't afford — and a lot of pure junk. We are impulse buyers with the *ability* to purchase things. The "credit trap" is just as devastating to middle class families as the "welfare trap" is to low income families.

The following list consists of specific suggestions that I believe to be beneficial in planning for the future, and practical ideas that led to happiness on a day-to-day basis. If a young person walked into my office asking for financial advice, this is what I would say:

1. Don't use but one credit card. If you have several, select one and destroy the rest. If you have several cards with small balances, get them paid off ASAP and cancel them all. Put yourself on a program of no more impulse spending unless cash is used. Don't use debit cards. Force yourself to take dollars out of your wallet.

2. Don't even think about getting cash advances on a credit card. Understand that before buying any big-ticket item, you could probably do without it, and you can save for it. Our great-grandparents had to save for everything, but everything they owned was paid for. If you are used to making the minimum payment on the credit card account each month, you are in trouble. You have no business even possessing a card because the interest will eat you alive. Interest is like driving on a freeway and throwing that much money out your car

window. We all need to help break America's addiction to credit cards.

3. Start a process of acquiring hard assets in some form, or savings in some form, no matter how little you have to work with. While it may not seem feasible to put money into a savings account, with the extremely low interest rates being paid at banks and with all money fully taxable, at least *some* of your money is being saved rather than all spent. It's good training. Keep in mind that the alternative might be to spend yourself into oblivion, just like the government. Having a plan, regardless how small the amount saved, broadens your mind to opportunities and possibilities in the future — like being totally out of debt and staying out of debt.

4. Assume that the only one who is going to be looking out for your interests in the future is you. Don't plan on assistance, and especially federal retirement money, thanks to our autocratic overseers, especially if you are under the age of 50. Assume that you will have opportunities at your younger age to prepare yourself for the future by carrying out a meaningful plan to succeed. Face the reality that America offers opportunities for people to accumulate, while the history of government seems to suggest it can only consume. It creates nothing, and individuals don't want a life of creating nothing.

If this fictional young person is still eager to learn from me, I might share with him some of the hard lessons garnered by decades of effort. This is my legacy — this whole book is, in a way. No one lives forever, and if I can leave behind a few nuggets of truth that uplift the human condition, that is what I want to do. So here is what I would continue to tell him to be aware of as he goes about his daily life:

1. Whenever a politician is discussing racial issues and the differences in the economic classes in America, he

is being blatantly dishonest while appearing to be the protector of the people. While he is trying to convince the public how concerned he is about our well-being, in most cases he is simply an opportunist who will do anything, deceive anybody, and make any statement to help elevate himself into a position of power. Honesty and ethics are usually not his strong points.

2. Get involved in politics in some manner. It makes no sense to stand by and let other people speak for you when what is being said is not in your best interests, nor the best interests of your area or the nation. Encourage people you know to be educated voters in elections, especially in federal and state races.

   I'm certain that many people take an interest in politics and even spend a lot of time talking politics. Unfortunately, many of them still don't bother to vote, or they vote based on bad information. You will find that once you are an educated voter you can encourage a lot of people not only to vote, but to cast educated votes. For years I have called people before important elections, asking them to vote and suggesting who or what to vote for and why. Also, people call me, wanting to know who to vote for in various races.

   Speak out at local forums against local entities that are trying to create pork barrel programs from the government. Remind everyone that those are our tax dollars and there are better ways to spend them than on needless projects.

   Attend local political forums, listen to candidates promise the financial moon to potential voters, and make them defend their broad-range promises or wild plans, which always require tax money from somebody or higher taxes on something. Remember that their motivations are probably not the same as yours.

3. Ask your local newspaper to run not only the initial story supplied by *The New York Times* or Associated Press, but accompanying articles from other sources.

Put the issue or event into context. When you read an article attributable to one of the two primary sources, you can assume biased journalism. To me, it is not ethical to continually and systematically attempt to destroy a political party or a person by presenting only one side. Media people should at least have the decency to occasionally contact someone to present an opinion contrary to one consistently being presented.

4. Face the reality that America is, and has been, on a spending binge that it cannot possibly maintain. Accept the fact that our so-called federal debt of some 8 trillion dollars is a phony number. Our unfunded obligations are somewhere nearer *at least 60 trillion dollars, and probably closer to 80 trillion dollars,* counting all the bonds that are outstanding (mostly held by people in other countries), obligations to Social Security recipients and retirees, Medicare, federal retirement plans, and probably Medicaid — all currently funded by employees and employers, not a Trust Fund. Current tax revenues and bonded debt are paying for the obligations we began many years ago. There is no reserve and we are living much longer nowadays, so America is being held up like a house of cards, tumbling once there is not enough new money to pay monthly obligations.

Although America is heading toward financial collapse, very little is being done to prevent it. We have all heard that an ostrich will bury its head in the sand rather than face a threat. As a nation, that is precisely what we are doing. Rather than face massive problems, we bury our heads in disbelief or inactivity or busyness, not even wanting to hear about them, much less deal with them.

It's important to point out that in the fall of 2007 there was only an occasional mention by any of our national politicians of our federal debt. For all practical purposes,

when the subject of national debt was even mentioned, the political opposition would attempt to discredit the person for even talking about it. In other words, federal debt wasn't important, almost a non-issue across America.

There was a related subject which got even less discussion: the unfunded obligations of America. For all practical purposes, nobody had any concerns. On the contrary, in 2007 I stated that America is and has been on a spending binge with unfunded obligations close to 80 trillion dollars.

So where are we now, as of July 2014? We now find that our current national debt is almost 18 trillion dollars. It's almost unimaginable to face the reality that the entire nation is now talking about a debt that has more than doubled in less than seven years. Keep in mind that the 8 trillion dollar figure of 2007 took the entire history of America to accumulate.

America now knows there are no reserves to fund national obligations, including Social Security. So much for the "lockbox" politicians discussed in an attempt to convince/con Americans into thinking a Social Security Trust Fund was alive and well.

In pure defense of the beliefs I had in these subjects in 2007, I want to point out that my fears concerning these subjects were considered far-out, perhaps scare-mongering, totally without merit. In other words, I had concerns that almost nobody was even thinking about, especially our national politicians.

I was discussing these matters with all of my political friends, business partners, and others. I told them where all these issues were taking America and that I had no confidence whatsoever that they would even be discussed in the near future. I can honestly say that I was the most pessimistic person I know.

Yet I underestimated the severity of these problems and the time in which major national financial issues would get even worse.

Just what are the unfunded obligations numbers being discussed today? It's now commonplace to hear national politicians say "at least 100 trillion." Other opinions place it at 110-120 trillion.

As I write about these subjects, I find that it's quite easy to intermingle words. For example, when I refer to unfunded obligations, I find that I might be inclined to use the term "unfunded liabilities." Just the fact that it's become easy to use the words interchangeably bothers me.

Chapter 11

Afterthoughts — People, Reality, and the Reader's Response

The sole purpose of this chapter is to encourage you as a reader to think seriously about several important matters as I have done in relating these scenarios to you, and then for you, and you alone, to form your own opinion.

We must first face the reality that in every situation we are dealing with people — individuals in every walk of life: rich or poor, young or old, regardless of education levels or employment status. We are taxpayers and consumers; there may be businesspersons among us. We are simply humans with emotions, needs, judgments, motivations, and values. As such, in the society in which we live today, we are constantly making decisions in how we run our lives, our families, our businesses, and our government. With these realities always in mind, I ask you to make an honest evaluation of your life.

Do you choose to live day by day, without any plan for your life, or make plans from five years into the future to perhaps all the way to retirement at age 65? In other words, is your one life on Earth worth planning for, or is it of so little significance that next month, next year, or 20 years from today don't matter?

Do you consider yourself smart enough that when presented with a logical rationale of the reality of issues important to your future, you are able to make a personal analysis of the issues presented?

If your analysis of those important issues which will have a dramatic effect on your life convince you that changes are necessary, would you make those changes?

If you were in a business in which a significant portion of your business income could be generated as the result of being involved in some type of federally funded or subsidized program, would you utilize that opportunity to its fullest extent?

It's my opinion that in almost all situations such as this, we being human beings, motivated by money and status and typical Americans wanting to utilize any opportunity, would in fact take advantage of that position. Would you?

What if you were a potential medical recipient of an elective surgery or some other medical perk, would you utilize it to the maximum extent possible, knowing that the choice was left up to you and the service was yours without cost? I think I might be inclined to use it; however, my belief is that such benefits are not there to be abused. In other words, I personally would prefer to see programs used only when there are no other options available. What would you do?

Have you ever sat down and tried to determine what is really valuable in your life? In other words, on a scale of 1 to 10, where do such things as your spouse, family, job, home, automobile, recreation, retirement, health, security, relationships, food, toys for any age, freedom, pride, ethics, religion, and perhaps self-respect rank on that scale? I strongly suggest you put yourself to that test. I have done it myself and found the results to be most interesting.

If I am correct in my analysis that America has obligations, unfunded, that total at least 60 trillion dollars and possibly as much as 80 trillion dollars, and that we are living longer as a people and there is no discipline in the management of the affairs of the nation, are you satisfied that the system will not self-destruct at some point in time? What position will you be in, financially, if the system fails?

Since we absolutely know without any doubt whatsoever

that our national political leaders have deceived, lied, connived, and conspired to fool America about the financial health of this nation, do you have any respect for those leaders? Will you continue listening to their lies and casting votes for them? Perhaps the best rule of thumb when considering who to vote for would be simply to plan on voting against the candidate who makes the most promises about all the things he wants government to do for you. In the strange event a candidate starts discussing real issues that need to be dealt with, rather than expanding government and existing programs, that's probably the person you will not only want to vote for but get others to vote for as well.

Name just one national leader who has made specific proposals to reduce the cost of government, or eliminate any agency that serves no purpose. Can you think of one? Can you think of any federal employee you know who is paid by the month and chooses to work late hours, or perhaps give up a weekend to supplement his Monday through Friday schedule?

Why are there so many Monday federal holidays, including those Monday holidays taken by the House and Senate? How can so many hundreds of thousands of federal employees close offices entirely so often, never have to stay late, yet somehow do their jobs? Could it be that overstaffing is the norm and many of those so-called jobs aren't necessary except to slow down or hamstring other functions? Can your business always operate on banker's hours and close at every opportunity?

In private industry and business, even the banks can no longer keep banker's hours. You must remember that we must produce to prosper in America. If we are putting money in the bank, we have got to make things happen. That's capitalism and free enterprise, and that's great. Don't you agree that those are what fueled the engine of the American economy for decades?

Will you also consider one other thing relating to this subject? Don't you know that unlike the private free enterprise system, the federal government has three big legs up on all of us? Those being the one with unlimited ability to tax, the only one who can print money, and finally, the one who can consume yet produce nothing.

I think after you have honestly analyzed what is happening in America, you will be able to decide how to relate to the governmental system under which we are living. Here is my challenge to you. Become a knowledgeable voter, study the issues, and listen at every opportunity to what national politicians of both parties are saying. Look at the trends in taxation, bureaucratic spending, and the proper role of the government. Check out your income tax form, your withholding statement, and your combined total tax obligations. If you really want to know what's happening in America, look at the 1040 Tax Guide irrespective of your personal tax bracket, examining all levels of income.

My last question to you is this: How would you define communism? This is how I describe it: Communism is the end result of a socialized economy that has been nationalized by the ruling leaders, giving the Communist Party the power to enforce its rule at some point.

America is now in a transition period in which the capital system and free enterprise are not being encouraged and our national leaders coerce us toward socialism. Daily we move further and further away from the precious freedom that our Founding Fathers gave so much to create and so many in the passing decades have worked hard to maintain and even died to protect.

I think as a general tendency, Americans do not concern themselves much with trends, even when important situations might be threatening our nation and even the world. A huge majority of Americans don't want to bother with objectively analyzing issues that might have radical effects on our economy and everything Americans have worked more than two hundred years to achieve. Yet how can we justify looking the other direction? America has moved to a situation in which it is now almost impossible to deal with our unfunded entitlement programs, massive national debt, trillion-dollar deficits in our national budget, runaway expansion of government programs, and constant attempts to divide America.

With that in mind, I want you to take a look at the following list of countries of the world and the makeup of their peoples. This information is taken from the 2014 *The World Almanac and Book of Facts*. It's a recap of nations starting on page 747 and continuing through page 853. I would also refer you to page 995 of the General Index. If you want to read about the subject of Muslims, it simply says, "See Islam." All I want to do is have you actually look at some numbers. *Stay with me and take the time to check this out. I guarantee you'll find it most enlightening!*

The first column is the name of the country followed by its population rounded to the nearest one tenth of a million, followed by the percent of that population that is Muslim. The last column is the number of Muslims in each of those countries based upon its population and the percentage of Muslims. (Keep in mind that the words Muslim and Islam are almost always used interchangeably.) In some cases *The World Almanac and Book of Facts* also shows the percent of Sunni Muslims and the percent of Shia Muslims in comparison.

Nation	Population (in millions)	Percent of Population That Is Muslim	Muslim Population (in millions)
Afghanistan	31	99% (80% Sunni; 19% Shia)	30,690,000
Azerbaijan	9	93%	8,370,000
Algeria	38	99% (Sunni)	37,620,000
Egypt	86	90% (Mostly Sunni)	77,400,000
Gambia	1.8	90%	1,620,000
Guinea	11	85%	9,350,000
Indonesia	251	86%	215,860,000
Jordon	6	92% (Sunni)	5,520,000

Iran	79	98% (89% Shia; 9% Sunni)	77,420,000
Iraq	31	97%	30,070,000
Kuwait	2.6	85% (70% Sunni; 30% Shia)	2,210,000
Kyrqyzstan	5.5	75%	4,125,000
Libya	6	97% (Sunni)	5,820,000
Mali	15.9	90%	14,310,000
Mauritania	3.4	100%	3,400,000
Morocco	32	99%	31,680,000
Niger	16.8	80%	13,440,000
Oman	3	75%	2,250,000
Pakistan	193	96%	185,280,000
Qatar	2	78%	1,560,000
Saudi Arabia	25	100%	25,000,000
Senegal	13	94%	12,220,000
Somalia	10	100%	10,000,000
Sudan	34	Almost 100%	34,000,000
Syria	22	74%	16,280,000
Tajikistan	7.9	90% (85% Sunni; 5% Shia)	7,110,000
Tunisia	10.8	98%	10,584,000
Turkey	80	99.8% (Mostly Sunni)	79,840,000
Turkmenistan	5	89%	4,450,000
United Arab Emirates	5.4	96%	5,184,000
Uzbekistan	28	88% (Mostly Sunni)	24,640,000
Yemen	25	100%	25,000,000
TOTALS: 1,090,100,000		92.86%	1,012,303,000

Here are some additional thoughts for consideration. As we think about our history as a nation, and even the history of the world, it wouldn't be a bad idea to again analyze where we stand. There's a common theory that history repeats itself. If that is true, we need to look back on the history of America and who our friends were and who our enemies were.

Since you have just reviewed populations of mainly Muslim countries of the world, I want to now show you the 2014 populations of other countries of the world. While the names of the Muslim countries might not have been as familiar to most Americans 40 or 50 years ago, I'm guessing the next list would have rung some bells.

Nation	Population (in millions)
Australia	22.2
Belgium	10.4
Brazil	201
Canada	34.5
France	65.9
Germany	81.1
Italy	61.4
Japan	127.2
North Korea	24.7
South Korea	48.9
Mexico	116.2
Netherlands	16.8
Philippines	105.7
Poland	38.3
Romania	21.7
Russia	142.5
South Africa	48.6
Spain	47.3
Sweden	9.1
Switzerland	7.9
Taiwan	22.2
Tanzania	48.2
Thailand	67.4
Ukraine	44.5
United Kingdom	63.3
United States	316.1
Venezuela	28.4
Vietnam	92.4
Total:	**1,914,400,000**

Surely the names of Germany, Japan, North Korea and Vietnam bring back memories. We fought wars, and we do not forget wars. The total population in 2014 of those four countries is 325,400,000, which is a total slightly above America's population. In addition to that, we had a cold war with Russia for many years. Russia has a population of 142,500,000, and things are now heating up with them again.

It's interesting to compare these total populations of all the nations in the world listed above with the number of Muslims shown above, 1,012,303,000. Bear in mind that we fought three wars with nations that currently show total populations of 325,400,000 people.

If we now go back in history, even for hundreds of years, why did attacks on nations happen at all? One of the biggest reasons was conquest. Perhaps one nation wanted to take over another nation simply to get additional lands. Perhaps the natural resources of the country to be taken over were needed, or the physical position in that part of the world was an advantage. The country being taken over could have plenty of things another country might desire.

There have been numerous cases in which the people of a nation had no choice but to try to overthrow an oppressive government, perhaps even guilty of ethnic cleansing as part of that oppression. There is no shortage of reasons why wars/conflicts take place. Conversely, in some cases the warring nations became close allies in the future. The best example is the United States with its current allies, Germany and Japan.

There's a term we are currently hearing in the news that really bothers me. It's being used in discussions of both American political/economic matters and also international conflicts. That word is ideology. I just happen to be of the opinion that if a person is totally committed to an ideology and that ideology is evidently the most important thing in a person's life, a significant conflict with someone who doesn't support that position could easily take place.

There are millions of people in this world that hate America and the system that created our way of life. Our religions might threaten them and will not be tolerated. Considering the huge conflict that exists in our basically Christian religion and the millions of others that despise what we stand for, we should recognize that *there's at least a billion people in this world that are totally committed to an ideology in conflict with a huge majority of Americans.*

I have spent time in many nations of the world. Some of those were fully developed countries and some were Third World countries. I have had many opportunities to see the daily lives of people in which entire communities had almost no modern conveniences, used burro-drawn carts instead of automobiles, and suffered with low employment. I have seen communities with homes that were made of mud or concrete with no doors or windows.

By comparison to many neighborhoods in American towns that we would generally refer to as poor neighborhoods or perhaps as slum areas, some of those places I saw in other nations wouldn't even be considered livable. All I'm saying is that many nations of the world can look at the most minimal lifestyle of American families and really think we are rich, even if that family is on welfare. It's very understandable that America could be a takeover candidate for many nations of the world, especially if their ideology supports such a notion.

Chapter 12

Ron's Prediction of America's Future

I'm a historian and have been my entire life. When I was a young father my kids would inform their friends to not ask me any question relating to history. "Don't ask Dad. He'll go get a history book or the *World Almanac*."

Over the years I began to study the history of nations, including economics, politics and their eventual outcomes. That study did not exclude trends, motivations of people and nations, lifestyles, natural resources, and forms of government, such as capitalist/free enterprise, socialist, Marxist, communist, etc.

It's always possible to forecast a nation's future by analyzing the factors just mentioned. The only thing that's difficult to forecast is the timeframe involved. When all the various factors are in place to cause the eventual correction to take place, it will happen.

With that in mind, I want to give you my predictions for the future of America after I quickly recap in a short list.

1. America and its people have never been more divided in our history. There's a daily attempt to intentionally divide our people based mainly on economics, but in addition, on race, ethnicity and

even sex. Some of our national leaders make attempts to incite envy and even hate among people.

2. America is witnessing political hypocrisy from national leaders whose sole intent is to keep them in their elected positions of power.

3. The huge majority of nearly all elected leaders are fully aware that there's an economic collapse that will take place in America.

4. Those political leaders absolutely know that, based upon national trends, business as usual cannot continue.

5. The reason America is not addressing problems is that many of our so-called leaders simply could not care less.

6. Throughout the history of America, for at least the past century, we have never witnessed such totally vile statements being made by elected people at the national level. We no longer hear "the honorable gentleman" or "gentle lady" as an introduction for our elected leaders when they speak in front of their colleagues. We now hear name-calling and even personal attacks against opposition party members. In some cases allegations were made — and had those same allegations not been made from the floor of the House or Senate, a lawsuit would have resulted, alleging slander.

With all this in mind, and knowing that we must look to the federal government to actually deal with monumental problems, here are my predictions, and why.

We will not deal with our unfunded liabilities problem, and here's why not. The total amount of money involved is so massive that it would require America to do the following things at a minimum:

1. Raise the Social Security tax to at least twice the present rate.
2. Raise the full retirement age for Social Security to at least age 70.
3. Admit to America that there is no lockbox for Social Security, and further admit there have never been more than 90 days of Social Security contributions on hand prior to necessary expenditures.
4. America must recognize that we have now become a socialist nation. There has been plenty of speculation that we are moving toward socialism, but the truth is *we are already there.*
5. Our unfunded obligations are so huge that we cannot fund them unless we dramatically devalue the dollar by printing trillions in new dollars. This will take place.
6. We cannot continue selling billions in treasury bonds each month, bonds purchased by the Federal Reserve by continually printing money, all of which is part of the Quantitative Easing Program.
7. America, due to our national leaders, will not make any meaningful attempt to reduce welfare programs. In contrast, we will qualify more and more people to be eligible to receive benefits. Please understand that I am not talking about more people qualifying because of population increases. The following is why.
8. We will see a huge increase in senior citizens qualifying as welfare recipients. They will qualify for the food stamp programs, subsidized housing and utilities, and for non-payment of the Part A and B

portion of the Medicare Health Program. There will be a huge increase in the number of senior citizens moving to Medicaid since there's no premium to be paid and no co-pays required.

9. We will see a huge increase in the number of people, including families with reasonably high incomes, becoming qualified for a multitude of federal programs.
10. There will be no meaningful reduction in federal programs.
11. There will be a substantial increase in the number of federal employees, along with increased budgets to fund those larger and expanded agencies.
12. The military budget will continue to be reduced to fund out-of-control programs.
13. We will witness a radical expansion of federal authority over states "in the public interest to preserve America." That expanded authority will result in states literally having no sovereignty whatsoever.

Here is my last statement about our probable future: The America as we have known it for decades will cease to exist. Our economy will fail. Our free enterprise/capitalist system has perhaps a one in 25 chance of surviving. We cannot meet our obligations even if we try. Even if the entire nation and its political leadership admit to reality and try to deal with it, the odds are stacked against us. There is no way we can pay more than 100 trillion dollars in unfunded liabilities, tell tens of millions of people that all the freebies are coming to an immediate end, that the nearly 18 trillion dollar published debt will actually be paid, or in the alternative, that inflation created by printing trillions in new dollars will be avoided.

Why in the world would I speculate that such a bleak future could ever take place in the United States with little chance of avoidance? The facts are that it has happened before, just not in the United States. Think about this as my last thoughts to close this chapter.

Germany, after World War I, had a huge debt. In a single day, Germany printed enough marks to pay off all the debt it incurred in its history. Prior to the start of World War I, the United States dollar was worth the equivalent of four German marks. I have in my safe, currencies printed in Germany in 1923, single notes dated October 1, 1923, in the amount of ten million marks, and notes dated October 15, 1923 in the amount of a hundred million marks. I have a stack of those multi-million mark notes. They are worthless. This dramatic shift has happened before, and it can happen again. All a nation, any nation, has to do is make the decision to print more currencies, in any denomination, to pay off debts.

Chapter 13

America Wants and Deserves the Truth

I have tried to explain the problems our country is facing by dealing with the important issues haunting this nation. I have done everything in my power to explain the vast complexities.

Before I relate the one, and only, way our national problems can be resolved, let's recap factors which have contributed to the problems, with some new ideas and suggestions intermingled.

At the end of this list, I will tell you why there's only one way that our national problems can be resolved. You may be shocked by the fact that I would actually propose such a drastic event to take place.

1. Our nation now has unfunded obligations that we cannot meet in the very near future, much less the distant future.

2. These unfunded obligations, if part of a publicly traded corporation, would be considered as liabilities that the corporation could not possibly fund.

3. It's quite likely that the officers in key positions of that corporation could be indicted for representing liabilities as being assets, or at a minimum, be held

financially responsible for losses incurred by stockholders, bondholders, etc.

4. America now has somewhere between 110 trillion and 120 trillion dollars in unfunded obligations, along with some 18 trillion dollars in debt.

5. There are so-called income-producing assets by the federal government that are actually debts and liabilities, such as the "interest" being paid to the Treasury on Social Security "contributions."

6. The bureaucracy continues to grow in size insofar as budgets are concerned, in the number of employees on the payroll and the scope of activities.

7. Welfare programs are totally out of control and getting worse every year. Rather than properly administering these multiple programs, we have people working within the bureaucracies that simply do everything in their power to qualify as many people as possible for whatever program or programs are available.

8. Welfare/direct aid/entitlement programs are now so attractive that millions of people have become fully aware that they can actually qualify for totally tax-free programs that result in more dollars in their pockets than they would bring in if employed. They choose welfare as a lifestyle.

9. We now have direct aid programs, which were originally created to meet some temporary situations, that have become not only permanent but increased in scope.

10. America has seen such a growth in programs, now evolved into ongoing national entitlement programs, that they are being considered a "right."

11. When talking with individuals or groups, I quite often end the discussion with this fact: There is a complete void in telling the young people of this nation about the American free-enterprise system. Our national leaders from both parties don't talk about what made America great — the opportunities for success created by working hard, getting an education, being creative, taking responsibility, taking pride in their work and their communities, and developing self-esteem.

12. America, as a nation, doesn't value the principles that made us what we became over two hundred years ago. Our free-enterprise system is now despised by millions of people and simply not participated in by millions more.

13. Our national leaders are *all* fully aware of inevitable situations, which absolutely will happen in the future.

14. The Federal Reserve's low interest program, which has been underway some five years, is a national disaster. This is the Ponzi scheme of all Ponzi schemes in the entire history of the world.

15. The facts concerning interest rates and our national obligations are as follows: I would remind you that in 1981 the prime rate went to 21 percent, and at the same time some corporate bonds were paying 15 percent. If we had to pay only 7 percent interest on our 18 trillion dollar national debt, the cost would be more than one-and-a-quarter trillion dollars per year.

16. If we faced the reality that our unfunded obligations were actually debts and that amount just gets bigger each year, and we had to pay 7 percent interest each year on, at least, 110 trillion dollars,

that would cost 7.5 trillion dollars each year in interest.

17. High inflation is on the way and it's inevitable.

18. The value of the dollar will likely diminish substantially in purchasing power and possibly crash.

19. The long-held belief that there's no limit to opportunity to succeed in America, and the motivation to becoming financially successful, will continue to slide.

20. More and more people, of all ages, will become totally dependent upon the federal government for their complete existence, especially older Americans.

21. The most important obligation of our federal government, to safeguard the freedom of America and its people, will be replaced by commitments to fund federal entitlement programs.

22. Federal authority will supersede state authority regardless of state laws. The effect will be the loss of sovereignty by states.

23. No matter what national leaders who oppose the direction America is taking say publicly, whether members of the House or Senate, they will be discredited by the opposition, most of the media, and simply not be given a forum in the printed media. In most media situations, they will be called names, accused of no telling what, and become victims of unscrupulous journalists.

24. There are literally tens of millions of people in America who have never actually taken the time to analyze the economic status of this nation and the gigantic problems it must deal with. They have no

idea that they will personally become victims of a predictable disaster.

Here's the only thing that can save this nation from a total collapse. I want to assure you that I have tried hard to not mention by name either the Democrat Party or the Republican Party — or any members of those parties. Yet I must do so at this time.

To me, this is the only way that the problems of America can hopefully be resolved. Nothing else will work, and any other plan would fall on deaf ears. *Here's what must happen:*

IN ORDER TO SAVE OUR NATION FROM A TOTAL COLLAPSE, A VERY SMALL GROUP OF NATIONALLY ELECTED <u>DEMOCRATS</u> MUST COME TOGETHER AS A COMMITTEE TO PRESENT A MESSAGE TO AMERICA. THAT COMMITTEE COULD BE THREE <u>DEMOCRATS</u> FROM THE UNITED STATES HOUSE OF REPRESENTATIVES AND TWO <u>DEMOCRATS</u> FROM THE UNITED STATES SENATE. THAT SMALL GROUP WOULD RELATE THE REALITIES OF THE DIRECTION THAT AMERICA IS TAKING AND OF OUR CURRENT AND LONG-TERM FINANCIAL SITUATION. UNLESS ACTION IS TAKEN NOW TO CHANGE THE COURSE OF OUR NATION'S FUTURE, THE TOTAL COLLAPSE OF THE UNITED STATES IS THE INEVITABLE CONCLUSION.

The immediate response to my suggestion, obviously, is why would national DEMOCRATS do such a thing? There's no question that party members who participate would find themselves blackballed by their party leaders, lose positions, such as chairmanship of committees, or worse. They would be discredited, called names and probably not even allowed to speak from the floor of the House or Senate.

What would be amazing, however, is the fact that this organized group would be given a forum, even if the media totally opposed the group or groups. *They would have the respect of the majority of the American people for having the honesty to tell them the truth.* Their political opposition would even respect them.

This would be such an absolutely unique event in American politics that it would create discussions across the nation by literally millions of people from all walks of life, ethnicities, income groups, political persuasions and ages. Finally, when those DEMOCRATS are up for re-election, they would all win. America wants to hear the truth from our national politicians, even though it might be terrible news.

Here are some of the items those Democratic Party members could enlighten the nation about:

- There is no Social Security Trust Fund.
- The 18 trillion dollar nation debt, in and of itself, is currently under control only because of incredibly low interest rates, which are still destroying retirement funds.
- The 110 trillion to 120 trillion dollar obligations of America are actually unfunded debts and are getting larger each year; as life spans increase, new programs are created and existing programs expanded.
- America is witnessing the world's largest Ponzi scheme by the Fed (engaging in a low interest rate scheme to keep the federal debt from already destroying our financial system).
- There is no way America can continue to fund out-of-control entitlement programs.
- Face the realization that tens of millions of people actually *choose* to accept an entitlement/welfare lifestyle. That acceptance is now being handed down in families from one generation to another.

- Admit that with the constant growth of the bureaucracy, federal control has reached the point that the sovereignty of states is threatened.
- Admit that with the constant effort to buy votes by expanding various entitlement programs, the most important function of federal government is in jeopardy, that of funding the military to *defend the freedom of America.*
- The final and most important thing this group of Democrats must do is relate, *in real numbers*, how much it will cost to maintain the current programs of government, and that it's *virtually impossible to do it.*

These political leaders would present the facts and the facts simply couldn't be disputed. Arguments against those presentations, regardless of possible name-calling or irrational statements, simply can't have any credibility when compared to the cold hard facts. The only possible party that could be totally discredited would be the politicians that were foolish enough to think the American public was stupid enough to believe their perpetual lies and distortions rather than the facts presented by those DEMOCRATS that were simply relating the truth.

About the Author and the Publisher

Ron Slover's first job was at age 7, shining shoes on the town square in Tyler, Texas. He was self-supporting by age 9 and helped his family by, among other things, cleaning yards and houses, repairing bicycles and scooters, and having a *Dallas Morning News* paper route. Between the ages 11 through 13, a typical day would encompass the morning paper route, school during the day, and work in a general store after school and on Saturdays.

In 1951, Ron's family moved to Amarillo, Texas, and he continued to clean yards and houses. In his junior high school and high school years he worked for a water company, driving a commercial delivery truck by 16. In high school he joined the Diversified Education program, working from 12:15 p.m. to 7:00 p.m. Monday through Friday, and 7:00 a.m. to 7:00 p.m. on Saturdays at a discount clothing store.

Ron was also in the National Guard for two years while in high school. Joining the Air Force after graduation, he attended classes at the University of Hawaii and the University of Arizona during those four years. After being discharged, he worked for the Fort Worth and Denver Railway for more than six years, with the last two years also incorporating a part-time job in a small Panhandle town where he was a news reporter for an Amarillo television station.

Ron moved back to Amarillo and worked for the State of Texas as Taxpayer Compliance Officer, also known as a field auditor. During that time, he continued to work as a reporter in the television station's news department on the night shift for five years. After that, he was a full-time television news reporter for six years before advancing as the station's Director of News and Public Affairs.

Never idle, Ron studied several years to become a licensed real estate broker and a licensed life, health, and accident insurance agent. He also attended Amarillo College at night, graduating with an Associate's Degree in Mid-Management and later teaching a money management program to college students. Next he trained with an Amarillo stock and bond brokerage company to become a stock and commodities broker.

Ron made two unsuccessful runs for United States House of Representatives and then got involved in a battle dealing with the natural gas supply for the City of Amarillo. He elected not to run for the third time.

Forming his own general securities company while operating his stock brokerage company and being a real estate broker, Ron continued doing part-time oil and gas leasing and financial analysis for local oil and gas companies. Deciding to work full-time as an independent oil and gas consultant, he founded an oil and gas company with two other individuals. They sold that corporation after nine years of operation.

Ron had already begun a smaller oil and gas partnership with another individual from South Dakota, which expanded with a second partner and operator living in the Oklahoma City area. He also continued to acquire oil and gas interests in his personal account.

Ron currently is a major partner in three oil and gas partnerships, a shareholder in an oil and gas corporation, owns a small oil and gas operation of his own, and owns an apartment complex and several houses in Amarillo. He owned and operated a small radio station for three years and sold it in 2005.

Ron married his childhood sweetheart, Ramona, a girl he met the first year after moving to Amarillo and who he first dated when he was 13 and she was 12. They have three wonderful children. One son works for Ron, and the other is a policeman. Their daughter is a paralegal in the Dallas area. And a grandson now works for Ron, learning the oil and gas business while completing his bachelor's degree.

Ron decided to write this book because of his concern about how the nation seemed to be changing from a capitalist country, encouraging people to engage in free enterprise, to something less than what the Founding Fathers intended. Since this book was physically written on yellow pads by Ron himself, without the use of even a recording machine, it was time-consuming but well worth the effort.

As to Ron's future plans, now at age 70, they are conservative. He has managed to accomplish every goal he has set in his business life and is now in the process of paring down some of his business interests to the point that he can simply manage his personal properties, such as oil and gas, minerals, land, and real estate.

He has absolutely no plans to seek political office.

Ron is now 77. He continues to work hard, as he has done since age 7. Having been financially successful and in a position to make a considerable amount of money each year, Ron continues with his decision to never seek or accept any political position.

Due to health issues, he now believes it really no longer serves any purpose to see how much money he can make since such a large percentage of that income goes to federal taxes. Success, in America, is despised by the federal government. Also, if a person is consistently successful, he becomes a constant target.

He wants very much to travel with Ramona to all of the locations they envision, including more cruises.

Finally, his last life goal is to have this book as widely read as possible so people will start thinking for themselves rather than falling for lines from self-serving politicians and bureaucrats.

To order books or contact the author, email him at Slovers1@Yahoo.com, or send mail to 4000 Julie, Amarillo, Texas 79109, or call (806) 358-9280. Make checks payable to Ron Slover. The cost per book is $9.99. Postage is $3.50

for the first book and 75 cents for each additional copy. Texans need to add sales tax of 8.25 percent. You can request books be autographed for no additional charge.

The cost per book of $9.99 is $4.00 less than the cost of the smaller *The Buffet Syndrome* in order to make it affordable to more people. The author and the publisher are more interested in reaching a wide audience than in making a profit. This book is a labor of love to save our nation.

About Path Publishing

Path Publishing began in 1993 and has published more than 30 books and other projects over the years. We tend to specialize in general and Christian nonfiction, poetry, biographies, and self-help. PathPublishing.com contains the works of many writers. In the past we have been listed in these publications and are approved for future listings: *Christian Writers' Market Guide*, *The Directory of Little Magazines and Small Presses*, and the September issue of *The Writer*, when they list publishers each year.